EMPOWERED *Soul*

180 Mindful Intentions, Reflections, and Practices to Help Women Develop Deeper Awareness and Capacity for Life's Challenges

Kathryn Cluff

Empowered Soul

180 Mindful Intentions, Reflections, and Practices to Help Women Develop Deeper Awareness and Capacity for Life's Challenges

Soul Roots LLC

ISBN: 979-8-9909940-0-3

Art by Camille Cluff
Editing by Powerful Impact (Deanna Geary) and Carrie Pat (freelance editor)
Proofreading by Shelby Rawson
Book Design by Transcendent Publishing

Printed in the United States of America.

TABLE OF CONTENTS

This book is dedicated to all women—
especially those beautiful souls whose paths
have been anything but easy.

ACKNOWLEDGMENTS

My deepest gratitude to …

My partner and best friend, Mike, for his loving and unwavering support.
My children for their courage and love.
My amazing girlfriends who always have my back and a word of encouragement.
Every student, client, mentor, and teacher who has shared their wisdom with me.
Life and all of the lessons she brings.

Special thanks to my daughter, Camille, for creating a beautiful sketch depicting the woman in my meditation who brought me light during a dark transition.

PROLOGUE

Once you are a member of "the call" club, you never forget that moment! My initiatory call came on July 7, 1998. The woman calling told me that my husband was in cardiac arrest and that I should get to the hospital immediately.

In reality, the first call could be assigned to just a few days prior on July 1st, when I learned that Don—my thirty-five-year-old husband, best friend, and father of our children—was in a plane crash. I was shocked and unable to comprehend the news. My mind was in a different world as I was up to my neck in numbers as I processed payroll for four family businesses during our busiest season. The mental shift was difficult. My mom was helping me, and upon overhearing the conversation, moved into action. We dropped everything and loaded up to make the drive with no chance of arriving immediately.

There was plenty of time for my anxious mind to imagine the details on the eighty-mile drive to the hospital. While my mom drove, I sat in the passenger seat, unable to breathe, occasionally glancing to the backseat where my three-month-old son slept peacefully in his car seat.

We arrived at the emergency room, and I entered alone while my mom tended to the baby. I was terrified by what I might see. Honestly, there is a void in my memory of what happened next. I remember speaking to our friend who was along on the trip as a passenger in the single-engine airplane of which my husband was the pilot. I felt terrible that he was injured—especially since he was an older gentleman.

He shared details about the crash, and I was baffled at how such a great pilot could have ended up on the side of a mountain. It had to be a mechanical failure. I would later learn that one of the fuel tanks, the one being used at takeoff, had run out. While fueling had been requested preflight, only one tank had been filled, and this was not detected until it was too late.

My husband suffered from chronic pain caused by a prior neck injury followed by an unsuccessful surgery a few years earlier. We used to make a joke that the surgeon's Rolex watch fell in during the procedure which is why he still had so much pain. On this fateful day, he was on his way to a doctor's appointment trying to find a way to manage his condition. The choice was to either make a quick flight or drive four hours to see this specialist. Flying seemed the best option at the time but turned out to be the worst.

While the hospital staff struggled to stabilize his precarious condition in preparation for spinal surgery, I would make the 160-mile roundtrip daily. Mornings and nights would find me with our four children, ages three months to seven years. Before the accident, all but the baby spent the days with their dad. I would take the youngest to work as I was nursing at the time. These sweet children were understandably upset at the news of the crash, and felt the overwhelming state of stress I was in.

I passed along what the doctors told me to family and close friends, which was that I better prepare my home and life to take care of my husband after the surgery. His recovery would be lengthy and uncertain. So, that's what I did.

The day for surgery came when the doctors would repair Don's spine—which was broken in two places—while simultaneously managing other wounds, internal injuries, and bleeding. I kept in touch with a nurse for updates with a plan to drive to the hospital to be with my best friend post-surgery. Unfortunately, this is when I received "THE CALL."

It was a stifling summer day as my mom drove while I sat in the passenger seat, unable to breathe, unable to move, and unable to glance at the baby sleeping peacefully in the backseat. My whole being was rigid, and I was fully aware of the absolute surrealism of the situation. *How could we ever survive if he doesn't survive?!*

On arrival, I ran the long route to the ICU while my mom tended to the baby. I began to slow my pace when I saw the surgeon standing in the hall waiting. My heart sank. I knew. A short time later, my mom appeared with the baby in the carrier. If the doctor looked upset when he saw me alone, his affect took a spiral downward when he saw the baby. He explained what had happened during surgery and how they did everything in their power to save him, yet it was not enough. He directed me to a consultation room, but I wanted to see my husband.

I cautiously entered the room where he took his last breath. Syringes and caps littered the floor, and I had a deep sense of the commotion that had taken place earlier. There he was, my best friend, husband, love, and father of four beautiful children, lifeless, worn, and still.

There was no longer any urgency. Why rush only to face the task of telling our two children old enough to have some level of understanding, that their father wouldn't come home again? Why hurry to tell friends and family that he was gone? All the world outside of this moment seemed to disappear. I don't recall how long I stayed, but eventually I emerged from the room on wobbly legs that seemed too weak to carry such a heavy heart.

Flash forward twenty-four years to 2022. My children are all grown, and I had become a grandmother—twice! Somehow, we had all survived our tragic loss, but not without scars and more loss. We had to say goodbye to my father and mother. And my father had also spent his last hours of life in the very same hospital just a few rooms away from my husband.

On June 18, 2022, there was another life-changing call. This time I initiated the call. After a day of searching and making several phone calls, this call was the one that revealed where my son had been. That baby, who all those years ago slept peacefully in the backseat, had been life flighted the night before to the same hospital as his father and grandfather. He had crashed his car, been ejected, and was barely alive.

It was a stifling summer day as my partner drove while I sat in the passenger seat. It was the same route, same hospital, same ICU, and again, I struggled to breathe. I called my other children with the news, barely able to get my words out.

We arrived to learn that his condition was precarious and that he would require surgery to stabilize his spine. He had a multitude of serious injuries. We were also informed that he would likely not walk again. As I looked down at him, I felt completely devastated, not sure if what I was seeing and hearing was real. I wondered if this was some sort of sick joke orchestrated by the universe.

My son would spend two more months in the hospital, followed by a month in rehabilitation. We made our first trip out into the real world in early September, wheelchair tucked away in the hatch of the car. This would be the beginning of a long line of firsts, most of which were scary and tense. It was nearly impossible to comprehend that I was being entrusted with his total care. But how wonderful it was to be home! May I not spend another minute of my life in a hospital! That is something we all agree on.

By the time this book is published, we will have been home, even have moved to a new, more accessible home two years ago. We have established routines and roles and have grown and overcome what once seemed impossible. We might be seeing light at the end of the tunnel as the darkest days are seemingly behind us. This is not to say that there aren't tough days. There are certainly those!

As I reflect back, I am in awe of my younger self. I give her credit for her incredible resilience and fortitude to maintain a tight grasp on hope throughout life's challenges. Am I boasting? No, simply acknowledging. She did the work of gathering powerful healing tools and I am eternally grateful.

These practices (those in this book) developed over the years after my husband's death, the leaving of my dysfunctional thirteen-year relationship that followed, and the deaths of my parents. Each experience motivated me to grow and equipped me to walk through this most recent trial with purpose and presence. Whatever lies ahead, I have faith that the woman I am becoming will face it with courage, compassion, and intention.

INTRODUCTION

When I began writing the following intentions, it was for the purpose of processing the overwhelming circumstances I found myself living in. I was also thinking about you and the mountain you may be climbing. I wondered how I could use my experience to help. May these words from the deepest parts of my soul inspire you.

There are eighteen collections in this book, totaling 180 intentions. Why? Well, honestly because 365 would have made the book too big. When I chose the number, I thought how a 180° rotation is significant as it turns us in the opposite direction. Believing that things land where they're needed, I trust it has a purpose.

These pages are filled with a variety of tools that I've collected and put to work along my life's journey. They have and continue to support me in dealing with hardships, finding inspiration, and experiencing deep growth and transformation. In my personal daily journal, I use a simple format that I call Intentional Journaling, which includes these four focuses: Intention, Release, I feel …, and Gratitude. A more detailed description is found at the end of this book.

You've likely heard the saying that "no one gets out of this life alive." It's also true that no one lives in this life without a swift kick or two to the posterior. Unfortunately, it's easy to believe that you're alone in your difficulties. The truth is that you are part of a greater collective of women in need of community, and when we conspire to support one another, we are so much stronger.

Often, the inspirations and answers needed are within you and only need coaxing to the surface. My writings are invitations or nudges to catalyze a gradual transformation of gently easing the grip of fear and grief deep inside, allowing it to float into the light where you can see it for what it is and move through it with intention.

I would like to offer a few suggestions for using this book as a tool that supports you through all of life's challenges, great or small. An essential and accompanying tool that will afford you the greatest benefit as you read is a journal. This can be a paper or digital journal, a notebook, a Word document, or an audio recording. Choose a format that feels good and doable.

Next, decide how you want to approach using this tool. You may want to read one entry daily or weekly—of course, this could depend on the topic. Maybe you're more adventurous, so you close your eyes, ask your heart what she needs, and open to a random page. You may even want to read the entire book once, then come back for a deeper plunge. Whatever you decide, I encourage you to take your time, read, and journal consistently, and make a ritual of meeting with yourself to do this important work.

These writings have helped me when I initially typed the words and multiple times through the editing process, and it is my hope that they will be a tool to provide encouragement, to remind you that you're not alone, and to empower you with lifetime skills for tapping into your inner badass.

I see you, honor you, and invite you to begin where you are, show up for yourself, and do the work of healing for your own sweet self.

COLLECTION 1

Expanding

The Emergence

Intention: Be open & creative
Release: Limitations

Today, the ideas that came to me while washing my face were those that stop flitting and floating and land solidly in the realm of true aspiration and inner belief.

Do you have days where you think anything is possible? Maybe I'm being naïve, but honestly, I don't care. The past months have been rough! I feel deeply grateful for this gift of an open door of hope and distraction from the harsh realities of the present. I plan to ride this wave of creative energy and see where it takes me.

We all have ideas, many of which are like dandelion seeds that drift upward on a breeze but become lodged in a tree or somewhere without soil to grow. But today is different for me. The seeds have landed on the warm earth of my heart, and I am watering them and bathing them in the sunlight of my attention. I'm excited because I know that where attention goes, energy flows.

Today, make a list of ideas that have floated your way and choose one to nurture by giving it your attention.

Surrender

Intention: Be open to ideas & welcome creative energy
Release: Self-limitations

My neighbors are getting new shingles on their roof today. As I watch the five men working together, each doing his part, I am reminded that much more can be accomplished when we come together with open minds and purpose. We cannot live a full and creative life in isolation. If that is true for you and me, I believe it's true for all.

I used to hide myself away, thinking that I was too different, or in many ways, not enough. One important fact I have learned on my journey is that such beliefs are far too common. It's true that each of us is unique, yet we all share the common bond of humanity. We are perfectly made as distinctive individuals to stand arm-in-arm in community for our highest, most creative good, and the greater good of all.

In the same way that a recipe combines different ingredients to create something delicious, by adding our personal gifts and unique nature to the world, we become a part of something.

So today, let your light shine brightly! Be your beautiful, authentic self. Know that you are needed just as you are because you are a very special ingredient in something greater!

What Is

Intention: Release, rest, and soak
Release: Attachments (to old beliefs, ideas, stuff)

It's Sunday—a gorgeous, sunny fall day. One of the few remaining 50° days according to the extended weather forecast. I have been taking advantage of the long fall, standing barefoot in the green grass to hang laundry on the line with snow patches still present in the shady spots.

My daily walks are filled with the season's earthy tones and the smell of damp leaves in the crisp air of late afternoon. Nature is releasing to prepare and preserve for the inevitable arrival and long visit of winter. She is slowing down. I feel her energy as it sparks my desire to release the mental and emotional clutter I have accumulated yet again. The need to wind down, rest, and breathe in the peaceful, healing air is palpable. After the squeeze of a chaotic summer, I'm eager to rest and soak in the quiet stillness of this new season.

Consider decluttering as an outlet for releasing your hold on attachments today. Take five to ten minutes to choose an old, worn-out belief, idea, or a physical item. Write what you have chosen on a piece of paper with an explanation of why it has to go. Then either burn or bury the paper. You can also place it in a glass of water. Whichever method you choose, your intention is to let go of your attachment. If it's a tangible item, select and carry out a method of letting it go. Now, it's time to rest and soak in nature.

Interruptions

Intention: Focus & breathe
Release: Intense energy

It's Monday, and I'm hitting the ground running. First, my practice on the mat! Next, I'm moving from task to task, working my way down a long to-do list. As I proceed, I feel tension building in my mind and body.

This would be a good time to pause and breathe, but I keep going. After meeting myself in this awareness two or three times, I resolve in my mind that I will not complete my agenda and accept that the "interruptions" that keep distracting me are actually the universe's nudges. Each is a reminder to find balance between a full sprint and pausing to check in with myself and take in the people and world around me.

We tend to be almost addicted to lists, schedules, and general busyness. It's often our way of feeling like we are a contributing member of society. It may make us feel useful and important, but at the end of the day, we are mentally, physically, and emotionally exhausted.

Practice seeing life's interruptions as the universe's way of looking out for your well-being. See each as a gentle, compassionate nudge to balance and release intense energy.

Shift

Intention: Productivity with ease
Release: Fear

When life is turned upside down and changed forever, fear can take up residence and follow us through the days like a constant shadow.

I'm in the aftermath of such an event, and I'm still looking around wide-eyed in a land that feels foreign. It's scary to think about what the future holds, so I do my best to keep my mind focused on the present. But when I succumb, my imagination creates shadowy figures like failure, loss, and sadness. In response, my body kicks into the stress response. I feel the thick, tense, and nervous energy weighing down my entire being.

I have a long list today. Same as yesterday. My go-to is to dive into GSD (Get Shit Done) mode, but I catch myself. Approaching my tasks from a place of ease sounds divine. I'm tired of stress! I sit, journal, and take full breaths.

Is it possible to be productive without running full speed and ticking off tasks from a list like a maniac? It is! Will we sink hopelessly into a sea of the undone by stopping to check in with ourselves, breathe, and rest? NO!

Today, practice being an observer of yourself. Notice how you breathe, move, and approach your responsibilities. If you find yourself in GSD mode, pause for a few minutes of stillness and focused breathing to give your nervous system a reset. This will shift your anxious energy to ease and support you to release the grip of fear.

Mind-Body

Intention: Hold space for abundance
Release: Feeling of being stuck

It's a blustery fall day with blue sky and clouds that foretell the coming weather change. I can feel the shift in my body as aches, stiffness, and a headache. My mood is dampened, and I long to be alone. But that is just not in the cards today.

My physical experience is impacting my perspective as my perspective reinforces the uncomfortable sensations in my body. It's a great example of how the mind and body are inseparably connected. As a way to support this relationship, I decided to pay special attention to my breath, my thoughts, and move my body with compassion and gentleness. I speak kindly to myself, expressing gratitude to my body for carrying me through this life. I will use the mind-body connection to my advantage, healing both mentally and physically through this practice.

Stress is a part of life, but how we process it is something we learn. The more self-aware we are, the more equipped we are to manage the process rather than being controlled by it.

As you stand solidly on your feet, bring your awareness to your body. Mentally scan from the crown of your head to the soles of your feet and notice the sensations. Do your best to be an observer rather than a judge. Take a second scan, and this time speak kindly to your body.

Abundance

Intention: Accept interruptions
Release: Demands

Here I am well into the afternoon and just now sitting to journal. I woke up late, had a limited yoga practice, and dove into the day. Responsibilities, deadlines, demands … and interruptions.

The demands are in the tone of my own inner voice. It questions why I don't have this done and that started. My days are filled with starts and stops queued by interruptions that are, at times, responded to with frustration.

My intention today is to hold each disruption with acceptance. I have decided to consider the source of each disturbance and honor the fact that I am needed by and trusted by others. That feels more like abundance than interruption.

As wives, partners, mothers, single mothers, breadwinners, cooks, housekeepers, and general caregivers, we can feel the only way to not be interrupted is to move to a deserted island. But let's hold off on packing our bags. While being disturbed can be frustrating and even exhausting, it's also a sign that we are important to others. Then again, it may also be that we need to set boundaries. Perhaps both?

Do you feel like your days are filled with one interruption after another? How could you shift your response to and reframe "interruptions?" Of course, there are things that really are interruptions, so arranging a "do not disturb" time is a great idea too.

Overthinking

Intention: Be in the flow
Release: Overthinking

For most of my life, I have struggled with anxiety and its annoying sidekick, overthinking.

Overthinking pulls me on a mental journey to the past and/or future where I feel disconnected and often afraid. But this intention to be in the flow is a gift of open space to experience the day and moments as they come. Living in the present requires my attention and thus draws my awareness to what is right in front of me. It's a place where I feel whole and engaged. It's also a place where I feel deep gratitude for the many teachers, mentors, and holistic tools I have been blessed to encounter.

Thankfully, there are a multitude of practices that we can implement to help us break out of anxious patterns.

So, when you overthink, here is one practice to begin retraining your brain. Each time you catch your mind reenacting old experiences or telling you stories that create stress, place one hand on your heart and one on your belly. Take a deep breath in and sigh it out. Either aloud or to yourself, say, "I am present and peaceful." Over time and with practice, this will become a habit that heals and empowers you.

Dark vs. Light

Intention: Gratitude soak
Release: Others' negative energy

It's a Saturday morning, and I am blessed to have both of my grandchildren visiting.

I'm a partner, mother, grandmother, and more recently, a caregiver. My newest role hasn't been easy—especially the past two days. I can't seem to predict where my son's good days or partial good days will fall. This morning, the energy was dark and foreboding. I knew I needed to protect myself and my own depleted energy level. Really, all I wanted to do was soak in the amazing moments with these beautiful, sweet children and save them in my cells to warm my soul when the next dark shadows appear. I ward off the negative using all my will and power and join a game of hide-and-seek, complete with giggles and silliness.

Too often, we miss the sparks of light by sinking deeply into the heaviness of difficulties. It's like stumbling around on a dark night and failing to look up to see the stars. We owe it to ourselves to guard our energy, even from those we love most. It becomes impossible to be a strength to others if we continually sacrifice our own joy.

The way to overcome darkness is with light. Soaking in gratitude attunes you to the sparks around and illuminates your inner light. So, shine brightly. Not only will you lift your own spirit, but your warmth and brilliance will cut through the darkness you encounter.

Temporary

Intention: Be the sky
Release: Dark clouds

A feeling of foreboding has been lingering in the shadows of my mind for a couple of days.

Despite its presence, I have allowed joy and gratitude space in the spotlight. The dark clouds in life can be confusing for me until I remember their true nature. Like emotions, they pass through blue skies, blocking out the light for a moment. They are temporary. One floats in. As it floats out of sight, another may take its place. During the space between, the blue sky is visible, and the light shines boldly.

In teaching meditation, I remind students that their mind is the vast blue sky while their thoughts are the clouds moving across. It is much the same with emotions. Attaching to an emotion is like harnessing a cloud and losing sight of the fact that we are the sky.

Try this meditation today. Find a comfortable, quiet place to sit. Close your eyes and focus on your breath in and your breath out. When your mind wanders (when, not if), acknowledge the thought, then let it float away like a cloud. Remind yourself that you are the sky.

COLLECTION 2

Surrendering

Approaches

Intention: Surrender to the flow
Release: Control

Day 1: I have decided to hold this intention and release for the week.

In my thinking, we have three choices in our approach to difficult times: try to control everything, play the victim, or surrender to the flow. I have tried each and find surrendering to be the most empowering and energizing.

In the times that I tried to control everything, I felt like a drill sergeant. It left me feeling irritable, angry, and continually planning what was next. It entailed leveraging every minute with the utmost efficiency and dragging others along for the miserable ride. Control is mentally living in the future.

When I have chosen the victim approach, I could be a real sad sack. The ploy is to whimper and feel sorry for yourself as a means of manipulating others. It didn't take long to suck the wind out of everyone's sails, including my own. This role focuses on past events and leaves one feeling weak and vulnerable. Neither controlling nor playing victim solves any of life's struggles. Each brings more heartache and can eventually chase away good people, good jobs, and good health.

This is why I decided to practice surrendering to the flow this week. This approach plays out in the present, right where all the good stuff in life happens. There is no pressure to control or manipulate anyone or anything. It does require awareness—of physical sensations, thoughts, words, and emotions. When (not if) I lose track, I gently merge back into the flow. There is compassion here. Kindness. Forgiveness. Acceptance of what is. Acceptance of who I am in each moment. Acceptance of others. There is peace.

Will you join me in surrendering to the flow?

Resistance

Intention: Surrender to the flow
Release: Control

Day 2: One definition of surrender is to release resistance. Inevitably, life throws hard pitches, and we swing at them with all our might. Personally, I have wanted to knock the crap out of a few struggles. I have often wanted to slam them out somewhere else in the universe where they couldn't find the way back to me. It can be so irritating to have my plans derailed by … life.

There were times I attempted to hide from problems. I was resisting. This is a strategy used to create a feeling of control. But are we really ever in control? Resisting is a way to say, "I don't like this at all, and therefore I don't accept it!" This unwillingness to accept "what is" becomes an obstacle to growth.

On the other hand, surrendering or accepting the current situation puts us in the driver's seat and unclouds our vision. Remember, we do not have to like or agree with something to accept it. With acceptance, we begin to see possibilities and solutions where there was once darkness and hopelessness. We replace attitude with gratitude. We allow ourselves to be in the moment, leave the past behind, and get excited about what the future holds.

What would it feel like to give yourself permission to accept one thing in your life that you are resisting? Take out a pen and paper or use a page in your journal. The activity is to write a permission slip to yourself.

Example: Dear Gorgeous, I give you permission to accept that you are single again. You are forgiven and are free to forgive your ex-partner. Please know that I love you and will take amazing care of you as you heal. With Kindness & Compassion, Self.

Internal Rhythm

Intention: Surrender to the flow
Release: Control

Day 3: What exactly is "the flow?"

My definition of flow consists of two parts. The first is my own internal vibration or rhythm. The second encompasses all external energies. By this definition, it is reasonable to conclude that flow is not a fixed concept. It involves a constant exchange and interconnection between internal and external energies.

Our energy is impacted by our lifestyle. This includes nutrition, sleep, exercise, how we see and treat ourselves, our thoughts, illness, and injury—among many other internal factors. The environment outside of us will also affect our energy to the degree that we allow. This includes weather, others' attitudes, pollution, relationships, finances, world issues, social constructs, and more. It seems complicated, and it probably is, but we only need to focus on our own internal flow. By aligning and balancing our own energies, we sensitize ourselves not only to how alignment feels but also to energies that throw us out of rhythm.

Looking back, I can see my own journey over the years of gradually adding one healing practice, then another, and another. It's much easier now to sense what feels aligned and what does not. I detect imbalances more quickly and seek to rebalance before I'm in trouble. This can also be called self-awareness. Finding flow takes a healthy curiosity about oneself.

Do you ever have days where you just feel off? This is self-awareness. When you have this feeling, get curious about the *why*. Ask yourself questions. Answer them as best you can. Journal what you learn from this inquiry.

Persevere

Intention: Surrender to the flow
Release: Control

Day 4: This morning was frigid at 3°F. It was cloudy, windy, and frosty with every surface covered in a fresh layer of snow. It was a perfect backdrop for my feelings of despair and gloom. I really believed that I had been putting effort into finding a new normal, laying a foundation for getting back into my life, and reviving my business. Yet, all I wanted to do was pull the blankets up to my chin and hide.

Since we came home from the hospital with my son, we have all been adjusting and doing what we think is best. There are good days and moments weaved between the dark days and moments. Right now, it all just feels dark and heavy. I am trying to be creative and figure out a way to work and earn in the midst of caregiving. My mind takes one step forward and one step back, which leaves me feeling stuck.

I haven't given up, so I decide to acknowledge myself for my dedication and tenacity. Then, I move from bed to mat and clear some of the heaviness. Next, I write my daily gratitude list, renew my commitment to surrender to the flow, and jot down tasks to complete today. I feel more motivated now. My mindset has shifted.

We all have tough days, weeks, months, even years. We have this in common. It's what we do with the challenges that either supports or stunts our personal growth.

Think about a time in your life that was difficult, but you persevered. Take ten to fifteen minutes to write about what you did to get through it, something you learned about yourself, and the experience in the process. The fact that you are here means you haven't given up. Acknowledge yourself for your dedication and tenacity. You're a badass!

Frequency

Intention: Surrender to the flow
Release: Control

Day 5: Why is it so important to surrender to the flow?

Flow is to be aligned energetically. Albert Einstein said, "Everything is energy and that's all there is to it. Match the frequency of the reality you want, and you cannot help but get that reality. It can be no other way. This is not philosophy. This is physics."

The frequency we align with becomes our frequency. The adage "garbage in, garbage out" is one way to apply this. It includes what we eat, read, watch, listen to, who we hang out with, our words, and much more. If we want to be fit, we align with things that produce that result—exercise, nutritious food, drinking enough water, getting the right amount of sleep, etc. If we want to feel joy, we nurture and love ourselves, smile, and forgive. If we want healthy relationships, we align with vulnerability, honesty, and open communication.

The opposite is also true. If we desire the frequency of kindness, we must avoid the energy of hate, meanness, and criticism. So then, surrendering to the flow requires our active attention to balance our internal energy first, and then match that with the reality we want.

Try this simple energy experiment: When you go out today (I love to do this when grocery shopping), make it a point to smile and make eye contact with several people. Feel free to say hello and/or ask how their day has been—especially the clerk. Notice how your energy feels to you and how it influences others. Most often, they will align with your frequency. Pretty cool, huh?

Lessons

Intention: Curiosity about what I learned from my intention this week
Release: Doubt

The house is quiet, mostly. The sun is streaming through the windows on this chilly November morning. It's a glorious finish to a challenging and frigid week. I'm contemplating what I learned from holding the same intention throughout the week. Here are a few things that came to mind:

1. It's really hard to release control. It's scary, vulnerable, and requires the utmost trust.
2. I try to control more than I like to admit.
3. I surrender more than I give myself credit.
4. I am much more at ease and more productive when I allow others to have their own life experience while I choose which parts of that support my own desired experience.
5. When I'm internally aligned, external frequencies that don't match the reality I desire feel abrasive.

There is so much more, but now it's your turn. Make a list of five to ten insights you had from the past week of surrendering to the flow and releasing control. Now, reward yourself with a cup of tea and kind words of acknowledgement for contributing to your personal growth and flow.

Support

Intention: Contemplate & explore what I need
Release: Interfering with others' growth in the name of protection

Something I learned in a Celebrate Recovery women's group I attended for two years is how to be with someone who is struggling and allow them space to have their own experience. It's uncomfortable and counterintuitive. I feel pulled to place myself between them and their pain. When it comes to my children and grandchildren, the desire to make their pain go away is even more difficult to rein in.

It is natural to believe the desire to protect is founded in empathy and compassion. I believe that's true. However, I also believe that each instance requires a closer look at how I am impacting another's life experience. If it supports them to face and find ways to move through their pain, great! If I coddle and do things for them that they can do for themselves, I take away their agency. I'm not referring to acts of kindness or things they cannot do for themselves. I mean stealing their opportunity for healing and growth.

Personally, my path of healing and growth has had stretches of heartache and pain. Through this journey, I learned things that built resilience and gratitude. I don't want to interfere with the experiences of those that are dearest to me. So, as much as it feels mean, I will hold space in those instances and just be there.

What I need today is alone time to contemplate my own pain and explore what I need for support. I will also be curious about how to truly support others. I challenge you to do the same.

Negativity Bias

Intention: Hold space for the best outcomes
Release: Any doubt or negativity

Are you familiar with the human negativity bias? It's real! We naturally gravitate toward the train wreck scenarios where shit hits the fan, and someone falls through the ACME holes of life.

Focusing on worst-case possibilities is part of our survival instinct, and we need it to protect ourselves from true danger. Not everything is unicorns and rainbows, right?! But not everything turns out bad either. The cool thing is that we can train our brains to look for the good. This is not a passive process. It takes work, but it's also a game changer.

We have an appointment today that I have been mildly dreading. Thus, today's topic of negativity. The office is sixty miles away, and it's snowing like crazy. As much as I would like to cancel and put it off for another day, I want to face it head-on even more. I also want to shift my outlook from "Let's just get it done"' to "Let's be present, gain as much knowledge as we can, and hold space for the best outcome." This is my intention and release for the day.

Are you dreading something? Have you already decided that it will not go well? Keep in mind that your imagination and innate bias may be far darker than reality. So, set an intention today for a positive outcome or at least an experience that will support personal growth. Turn this intention into an affirmation to repeat periodically throughout your day for weeks or months and hold space for however long it takes.

Letting Go

Intention: Forgiveness and self-compassion
Release: Lingering energy from yesterday

Do you know those encounters that leave you shaken up and confused? I had one of those experiences yesterday afternoon.

It has been hard to release that sticky, heavy energy. My intention yesterday was to hold space for the best outcome for something I've been dreading. During the most intense part, I came back to this intention in my mind and thought, *WTF is happening?!* But I held to my intent and continued in the experience. Eventually, it turned around and became a relatively productive time.

Today, I will continue to release the emotional remnants and work toward forgiveness. I will be gentle with myself and not critical, as if my skin isn't thick enough to endure another's anger directed at me through intimidation, arrogance, and disrespect. That's their shit, and I have my own to sort out. Don't get me wrong, I will not subject myself to this person again. But I will forgive and release this energy for my own growth and well-being.

Are you carrying the heavy burden of resentment toward someone? If so, I invite you to join me today with the intention of forgiveness and compassion. Let us together begin the journey of letting go of that burden no matter how long it takes. Our well-being depends on it.

Transitions

Intention: Be present in transitions
Release: Self-judgement

To be honest, winters are hard for me. It's not just the cold, snow, ice, and dark skies. It's all of those things *plus* the emotions they elicit.

I'm sitting beside a large self-watering grow box I brought inside before the freeze. It's filled with vibrant mums of lavender, yellow, and dark purple. They are the brightest among the plethora of greenery in this room. I look forward to seeing them each day. Aside from my desire to save every living thing from succumbing to winter by dragging it into the house, they represent life and hope in this landscape of seeming death. Only it's not death. It's just a season that transitions into the next season.

For the past one-and-a-half years, my body has been preparing to transition from childbearing season to the next season, menopause, of which I have no familiarity. My stamina is low, and my body feels like a stranger. Maybe I can fix myself with a string of demeaning words. No, I want to support this magical and miraculous process by being present and compassionate.

Today, I will spend extra time in savasana or corpse pose. It has also been called "mini death" and is a time to embody what has been experienced on the mat *and in life*. I will begin releasing what is dying so there is space for this incredible transformation and new season to come.

How about you? Is there a behavior, job, relationship, or something in your life that you feel has reached the end of its season? How can you get on board with the transition and create space for what's next?

COLLECTION 3

Caring

Finding Center

Intention: Ease and flow
Release: Blocked energy

It's really no fun to feel off-balance. Although the past five months have completely turned life upside down, I have felt unbalanced for the past two years.

I have searched and experimented with various possibilities to support myself financially by doing something that feels creative, purposeful, and soulful. Ideally, I see myself teaching and guiding others to heal themselves. I've tried different approaches, yet it still feels like I'm missing a piece of the puzzle.

Picture a pendulum slowly swinging in and around a center point. Imagine the cord is made up of many strands, each an aspect of your being—physical, mental, emotional, and spiritual. When any aspect of these areas is out of balance, it may cause the pendulum to swing wildly or block any movement at all. Depending on the day, we may feel blocked or feel the need to reel in the wild energy.

I sense it's time to focus on releasing the trapped energy and/or gathering together what is scattered. Maybe this is where I discover the missing puzzle piece. Maybe this is how I regain a feeling of balance where all the strands become one strong cord at the center of my being. And so, I will continue my mission to merge into internal ease and allow my energy to flow. What I know for certain is that what I'm searching for is within.

Today, I will take a couple of breaks to sit, breathe, and tune into my own being. I will ask my soul if there is something she wants to tell me. I will patiently wait and listen. I encourage you to allow yourself a couple of five-minute breaks today to do the same. A short-term benefit is the release of blocked energy which will leave you calmer, clearer, and more productive (ease and flow). The long-term benefit is the gift of knowing yourself more deeply.

Self-Care

Intention: Pause for self-care
Release: Blocked energy

As my body works through the transition to menopause, I recognize that I need more compassion, less doing, and more being.

For most of my adult life, I thought breaks were for wimps. That is until one of my greatest teachers who, without a word, taught me to rest when I needed rest and also became one of my dearest friends and my adventure partner. She was exuberant, energetic, and always ready for a hike.

Over the years, we traveled together, hiked new trails, protected and cared for each other, and made new friends along the way. But she always took time to nap, especially as she aged. She's been gone for two years now, but her example of self-care has stuck with me. This sweet and wise girl's name was Spocky. I learned many lessons from her example during her short eleven years on this earth. As you likely surmised, Spocky was my loyal four-legged bestie.

Today started as usual with my yoga practice. After caring for others, I will go for an adjustment from my chiropractor. Then it's off to a late lunch with family. Later, I'll treat myself to an hour of dabbling in a new self-care practice: Qi Gong. A hot bath before bed will round out my day of focusing on self-care and clearing blocked energy. I feel better just anticipating!

What is one thing (or five!) that you can do to show yourself love today? Schedule it! Put a reminder on your phone. When that notification sounds, pause for self-care.

Self-Encouragement

Intention: Encourage
Release: Future

There are learning experiences that appear suddenly, smack us in the face, and we think, "Oh, I get it!" We take what we've learned and move on. Other lessons linger over weeks, months, and years. The thing is, we don't know how long we'll be in the trenches. I've always said that I can do almost anything if I know upfront how long I have to do it.

I fell in love with mountain biking when I was about thirty years old. I participated in a few timed events that each had a set distance, marked course, and a maximum time to finish. When the hills were steep, the weather was hot, cold, or rainy, the equipment failed, I crashed, or I was running out of steam because I knew how far I had to go, I paced myself and kept moving. I had prepared for it. I anticipated the finish line, a cold beer, food, and exchanging war stories of the ride with friends.

Unfortunately, we don't get such details from life events. We don't know how long, how far, or how much energy we need for the journey. In my thinking, difficulties can be likened to the saying about fish and house guests, in that they start to stink after three days. While guests move on, there are challenges that linger and stink up our entire lives if we let them. Relationships can sour, our disposition may become unpleasant, and we need to break up long-term difficulties by planning something to look forward to. It's like giving ourselves the gift of encouragement.

If you don't have a journal yet, treat yourself to one. Write a list of things you can look forward to short-term (daily, weekly and/or monthly) and something cool you can anticipate long-term (months ahead). Schedule these activities. Make plans with someone special. Look forward to the freedom and joy of indulging in an uplifting activity. Be present to soak in these encouraging experiences.

Four Agreements

Intention: Let the light in
Release: Old mental programming

For the past seven years, I have been diligently reprogramming my own brain!

My thinking was so skewed by fear, insecurity, and anger, which left me in a regular state of stress. After getting my ass kicked enough in life, it occurred to me that just maybe I needed to change. I started journaling daily. My writing became a way to vent, reflect, and practice vulnerability. It was hard to see myself fully, raw, seemingly weak, and deeply flawed. But there it was in black and white, all the ways I sabotaged my own happiness and well-being. As painful as it was, the process allowed light to shine in as rays of hope. I was determined to override the old, worn-out stories and begin writing something wonderful.

I've noticed that my most recent challenge has put me to the test. A part of me longs to hide away and say, "Fuck this! This is not what I signed up for, and I'm done!" That kind of talk is a fragment of old programming. But I'm no longer that person. I have overcome so much, and my new story is filled with hope and mostly healthy ways of coping.

One of the most impactful books that supported me in transforming those old lies was *The Four Agreements* by Don Miguel Ruiz. I learned that I have the ability to create my own reality.[1] We all do. We generate the stories and tell them to ourselves and others over and over until they are truly our reality, whether positive or negative. We must choose wisely.

If you haven't read *The Four Agreements*, get a copy and read it right away. Then, read it again. Write the agreements in your journal and repeat them out loud daily. This is the beginning of your new programming and the start of your new story.

The Four Agreements:

1. Be impeccable with your word.
2. Don't take anything personally.
3. Don't make assumptions.
4. Always do your best.

Speak Your Truth

Intention: Open communication
Release: Playing it too safe

I'm new to the role of caregiver for an adult who is also my son. We're cruising in on six months of this nightmarish experience, which included two months in a hospital, one month in rehabilitation, and three months back at home.

This has been the most difficult thing I've ever encountered! The days go by too fast, and important conversations are kicked on to the next day or week, and on it goes. We've been walking on eggshells, tiptoeing around my son's anger and regular statements about hating to be alive. This past weekend was very dark, and I was sucked into that energy.

My partner and I talked about this and, more importantly, talked about next steps and solutions. This morning, I came in with love, compassion, and firmness. There's no need to sacrifice joy for anyone, especially when it's in your own safe space—your home. There's no justification for someone treating you disrespectfully, blaming you, and spewing out ingratitude. There's also no benefit in coming in hot with a fury of sharp words. Nothing good can come from that approach, especially when the other person is in the midst of such a traumatic experience and is hurting.

If you're in a similar situation, I suggest sorting through your own emotions first, then initiate open communication. Communication is not only speaking your truth with love, but also listening with compassion. It takes courage to have such conversations. What it doesn't take is ego. Egos do not like to negotiate or seek compromised solutions.

Where are you playing it too safe and not speaking your truth? Are you part of a relationship that is valuable but strained and you feel like you're walking on eggshells? Today is a good day to initiate open, loving, and compassionate communication. You've got this!

Prioritize

Intention: Productive flow
Release: Overdoing

I have this habit of making a giant-ass list of to-dos on my phone calendar and then feeling overwhelmed as one notification after another pops up. It's more than any normal person can do. I make the list the day before with great enthusiasm which morphs overnight into "What the hell is this?" by morning.

Today, my rational self will pare down the list yesterday's overzealous, crazy woman made by prioritizing the three to five most important tasks, eliminating nonsense, and creating bite-size, doable steps. This will replace my counterproductive overwhelm with a satisfying, productive flow.

Do you make unrealistic lists that stress you out, too? Today, prioritize the top three to five tasks, forget the rest, and roll up your sleeves.

Magic

Intention: Spaciousness & synchronicity
Release: Not acknowledging the magic

Would you agree that we each have special contributions to make in this life?

I've been able to come to some realizations and insights about this concept recently. Of all the millions of possibilities available for any single event, many thoughts, decisions, actions, and countless other factors land us on the one path that aligns us with our unique and personal experience. Random? I don't think so!

Life is a long if/then statement. If I drink enough water each day, then I will be hydrated. If I am hydrated, then I will have better digestion. If I have better digestion, then my immune system will be stronger. Or, if I had left for home earlier or later, then I wouldn't have crashed into the deer crossing the highway at that precise moment. My examples are oversimplified because we all know there are many other factors I didn't include. But it's quite magical how infinite possibilities of "if" become finite possibilities of "then."

Today, I will bask in the spaciousness of infinite possibilities and how all things connect in a specific manner that gives form to reality. I am in awe of the magic of these synchronicities. If I believe that things happen for a reason, then I will learn from every experience.

I encourage you to actively look for synchronicities throughout your day. Do your best to keep an open mind and heart. If you do this, then you will experience the magic.

Being Present

Intention: Be present & gentle
Release: Feeling stressed

After setting my daily intention hours ago, I paused from cooking for Thanksgiving festivities to take a peek because in the hustle, I'd already forgotten. My morning self knew what she was doing! Here I am buzzing around the kitchen, feeling stressed by what still needs to be done by 2:00 p.m. It's currently 1:00 p.m.

Holidays can be magical unless we smother them with an attitude of GSD (Getting Shit Done). As I type, I'm taking deep breaths and reminding myself of what's really important. For me, it's relationships and being present to enjoy friends and family and showing them I love them by being present and gentle. Ten minutes ago, I was ramping up to irritation. That doesn't feel like love to anyone and feels terrible in my own body. I've switched gears thanks to the wise intention set by my morning self.

I've been setting an intention each morning for years and have set the specific intention to be present many times over. When I feel anxious and tense, I recognize these as symptoms of being disconnected from the present moment. Plus, I find there is always more to learn about my own behavior, and this provides an opportunity to practice self-awareness.

You can practice self-awareness today by carrying the intention of being present. Add it to your phone with reminders throughout the day. When the notification comes, pause, take a deep breath, and state, "I am fully present."

Daily Practice

Intention: Soak + Love
Release: Missing self-care

Yesterday was Thanksgiving, which we enjoyed at my brother's and sister-in-law's home. Today, we are preparing a second feast to share with our children at our home.

Once again, we started our day in the kitchen. My partner and I are both committed to our morning yoga practice, which we managed yesterday, but today, we had less time and decided to combine a walk with stops for chanting, breathing, meditation, and postures. The sun was warm on this unseasonably 50° day, and we used our hour to soak in the weather and scenery and check in with one another. It was absolutely refreshing!

Afterward, we rolled up our sleeves to finish cooking as family arrived. The conversations flowed. There was plenty of laughter as we shared stories and a wonderful meal together. To think that we could have cheated ourselves of self-care time! We had it all, and despite the busyness, we managed to maintain our routine of self-care, plus soaked in the blessings of the day.

The holidays can be stressful if we allow them to be. If this is how you have been experiencing them, I invite you to give yourself the gift of self-care—a hot bath, a walk, curling up with a book, etc. It's even more important to practice self-care with the added tasks of the season. By doing so, you will create the space needed to connect, soak in the special moments, and spread love.

First, TLC

Intention: Recovery & preparation
Release: Expectations

Sleeping in this morning was glorious! Is it still deemed sleeping in if you were up well past your bedtime?

The past two days of Thanksgiving were incredible, but today I'm weary. With a cup of coffee in one hand and a can of hot water in the other, I head to my mat. My plan is to listen to my body and give her exactly what she needs to recover. Preparations for a vendor event this evening will follow. First things first!

I have decided to keep my presentation focused to avoid overthinking. I will not place unrealistic expectations on myself in the space and time of the event. It is my first year at this venue, so I really don't know what to expect. I will stay open to whatever has drawn me to be present. I will trust my intuition and be prepared to offer my gifts to those whose paths cross my own.

For now, I need time alone to give my mind and body a dose of TLC. This is especially important as I will be sharing my energy with those who are weary from their life's journey.

Do you care for others? At home? At work? Please remember that this caring becomes a greater joy when you first care for yourself.

COLLECTION 4

Tuning

One Hour

Intention: Rest & recovery
Release: Agenda

It's a Sunday following three busy days. My energy is low, and my body is tired.

I treat myself to sleeping in and hanging out blissfully for an additional hour. This is out of the norm for me, being a caregiver and having a small business. As much as I want more of a routine schedule, I also tire of schedules. But it's time to get my son's morning routine rolling. Afterward, I'll hit the mat to gently move energy around my weary mind and body.

By the end of the day, I enjoyed a three-mile walk, cleaned bathrooms, washed laundry, and made a giant pot of soup. Can you see yourself in this scenario? I know I'm not alone in how I derail my best intentions to slow down and rest—just for a day! And even though I didn't technically give myself an agenda, I creatively lived one. Hmm. Maybe we can work on this together.

Join me this week in picking one hour on the day of your choosing to rest and recover. Wednesday from 1-2 p.m. looks good to me and I've added it to my calendar. How about you? Day? Time? Let's do this!

New Day

Intention: Begin again
Release: Last week's priorities

Ah, Monday is here again and has begun peacefully.

I'm motivated and looking forward to coffee with one of the most wonderful women I know. She's a friend who has become a sister to me. I'm excited to see her beautiful face and catch up. Together, we will schedule a series of sessions to boost her immune system. I'm looking forward to creating a program to address her needs.

My energy is still buzzing after our visit. What an amazing beginning to the week!

Before bed last night, I wasn't that impressed with my ability to stick to yesterday's intention of rest and recovery. I'd score myself at about 65 percent. Meh. But today, I release all judgement and everything I thought was so important last week. It's a new day, a new week, and a fresh opportunity to start with a renewed commitment to rest in between other, more taxing responsibilities.

How did your day start? Your mood? Were you stressed before your feet hit the floor? Give yourself permission to begin again. Tell the pushy, naggy inner voice that keeps reminding you of what you didn't do yesterday or last week to jog on. Speak it out loud. Really, tell her to get lost! Give yourself moments of rest between your more energetic priorities. Let today, and each day, launch with a clean mental slate.

Warning Signs

Intention: Listen for messages
Release: Over-ing (thinking, doing, researching, etc.)

I have spent hours here and there over the course of a week, researching a new dishwasher.

First, I narrowed it down to two, then finally settled on the one that would solve all of my dirty-dish problems. I headed to checkout, and entered my credit card information, only to receive a message that my card's expiration year was incorrect. What?! I'm holding it in my hand, and it's right.

After three more attempts, it occurred to me that maybe my perfect choice wasn't my kitchen soulmate after all. That wasn't the first technological glitch either. I blew past the others without blinking an eye. Alas, I decided to review the product details again and discovered the depth is an inch too much.

On the one hand, I give myself kudos for my dedication and focus on finding a suitable replacement, as dishwashers have changed over the past twenty-three years. (Yep, our old machine is like family.) Although I won't be adding the new machine as a beneficiary to my life insurance, I do hope for a long-term relationship. On the other hand, I must stop over-ing and just buy a damned dishwasher!

We can run into roadblocks whether we spend minutes, hours or days researching before making a choice. This is wise until it develops into a state of over-ing. There are enough hard decisions in life. Let's not overcomplicate the simple ones.

In the instances where we become locked-in on a decision, it's easy to ignore possible problems. When obstacles pop up, we might find them annoying and miss that they are warning signs. This is when we do well to stop, look, and listen. What is the message?

Relationship vs. Being Right

Intention: Encourage, but let go
Release: Others' decisions

Well, yesterday took a sharp turn that slowed overnight, then started again this morning. Confusing? It is for me too.

Spinal cord injury is new for us. I take my responsibilities seriously, especially when it comes to caring for another person's health. Even so, there is a line where I stop to respect their autonomy. Believe it or not, I can't always know what's right for myself, let alone someone else, and I'm even wrong sometimes (sigh). But this does not keep me from encouraging what seems best.

Mentally and emotionally, we were primed for another stint in a hospital until my son made the executive decision not to go. So, after dropping a specimen by the doctor's office, my partner and I took a quick walk in the chilly wind and landed at a local coffee shop. We are treating ourselves to uninterrupted time to process the current state of affairs and get a little work done. It's possible that we'll still end up at the hospital, but for now, we honor his decision and carry on.

Do you think you're right about the path someone you love should take? Do you push hard to get them to see it your way? This can be very damaging to relationships, as I'm sure you know. A wise yoga teacher once asked this question, which I often ask myself: "Do you want the relationship, or do you want to be right?"

Today, try to be encouraging. Kindly share your opinion once and let it go. Hold space for others to decide what's best for them and kindly support them.

Grounding

Intention: Transmute anxious energy
Release: Anxious perspectives

I awoke concerned that I had overscheduled my afternoon and evening. This thinking may have been fueled by the past two days of not knowing how serious my son's symptoms were. We received part of the answer, which we started treating yesterday, but my body is still in the experience today.

After plotting my day and hoping my interruptions will be minimal, I still feel the pressure. We didn't have time for asana this morning, and it looks bleak that I'll get back to the mat before 8 p.m. So, this tension will need to be moved another way. I decided to do what I can to push this energy down into Mother Earth and allow her to transmute the chaotic into calm. From head to toe, I will be a willing participant in this magic by using my attention and breath in the exchange.

Take a couple of moments out of your busy day to stand firmly on both feet, close your eyes, and bring on the belly breath. Make the peace sign with both hands (prana mudra) and point your index and middle fingers toward the earth with your arms fully extended at the sides of your body. With each breath in, pull down busy thoughts. With each exhale, draw calming energy up from the soles of your feet to the crown of your head.

Alignment

Intention: Easy productivity
Release: Tension

It's a frigid, snowy Friday after an eventful week. You know the kind of week where you're not sure if you accomplished much aside from the absolute essentials. But this day has the inherent potential for peace and knocking out a few responsibilities.

Yesterday, my body was adjusted by the chiropractor and today, I'm realigning my mind by focusing on one task at a time. This approach seems simple in theory, but in practice can be challenging.

My parents' generation were multitaskers and proud of it! They didn't draw attention to their hard work and long days. But in my generation, we often brag about how much we can juggle. It has been proven that multitasking isn't really possible, plus the attempt sends our nervous system into high alert. Over time, we wear ourselves out, creating an internal environment that is susceptible to health issues. Is it really worth it?

Sit or stand with me. Close your eyes. As you inhale, raise your arms above your head, bringing your hands together in prayer. As you breathe out, lower your prayer hands to your heart. Repeat two more times and on the third exhale, place your palms over your heart. With your hands still in place, repeat this affirmation two to five times: May I be filled with ease. Take this process with you today and repeat it as needed to reduce tension and fuel productivity.

Extreme

Intention: Complete three tasks with ease
Release: Self-criticism & irritation of not getting "anything" done

Extremes! "Nothing, everything, always, and never" are just a few words we throw out to drive home the seeming fact that all is lost. Life is crashing all around, and devastation is at hand!

I know it sounds ridiculous, but this is where I have landed. If I had a dollar for every time I have thought or said, "I didn't get anything done today," well, I'd be loaded. It's not that I wasn't productive, more so that I failed to tick much off my list. And I love to check things off because it feels like giving myself a pat on the back.

My goal today is to complete three tasks without judgment, without qualifiers (such as needing to be on my to-do list), and with an easy-going attitude. I will also use this affirmation throughout the day: I feel a sense of satisfaction with every task I finish.

When our inner critic is hurling extreme words around, it's time to sit her down for a chat. It's unlikely that a day goes by when we fail to do anything. Believe it or not, resting is something, and for many of us, it's more challenging than staying busy.

Would you be willing to join me for today's goal? Three tasks. No judgment or qualifiers. Easy-going approach. Affirmation. Ready?

What You Need

Intention: Ask for & give myself what I need
Release: Resentment

I've noticed (again) a theme running through my life. It begins with irritation and builds to resentment. The result is a voice in my head that says something like, *Whatever! I'll just do everything myself!* I heard this voice speaking loudly today as I hurried around taking care of essentials so I could get out the door on time for my granddaughter's birthday party an hour's drive away.

But, when I was alone driving, I heard another voice calmly nudging me to ask for what I need. I was grateful for the rational advice but also felt like a real turd for falling back into the passive-aggressive behavior I've worked so hard to overcome. I'm reminded that I'm not surrounded by mind readers. There are occasions when I find it difficult to simply ask for what I need. At times, it feels like I'm burdening others with my neediness or asking for things I can do myself.

Going forward, I'll practice communicating as soon as I notice the slightest twinge of resentment. I'll do my best to be brave by opening up a conversation about how I'm feeling and what I need to feel supported. I will do this as a way to show love to myself and to those closest to my heart.

As women, we are nurturing caregivers and can often pull off an amazing amount of work. Unfortunately, this can be at the expense of our own happiness and health. The reality is that our loved ones probably don't have that expectation of us. Likely, they are more realistic!

Today, pay attention to your internal narrative. If you detect any resentment, consider how you can kindly communicate how you feel and what you need for support.

Boundaries

Intention: Set hours
Release: Distractions

I've committed to a small social media gig where I will write content to post a few times each week. I do this for my own business as well. I have taken on a one-on-one client and am writing a customized twenty-week program for her and a six-week program to teach in my community in February. I also teach an in-person yoga class weekly.

These are things I really enjoy. But they must be weaved into the open moments between caregiving and nurturing all my relationships, including with myself. These limited and sporadic moments then need to be strung into productive hours to meet my responsibilities.

It all feels doable with some planning! How's that for a Monday morning attitude?!

My first relationship that needs better boundaries is with myself! I am gifting myself a bedtime and wake-up time. For the next part of this plan, I intend to carve out one-hour increments where I will work in a "no interruption" zone, barring an absolute necessity or emergency. Both impact others, so I will share my plan and my needs with them and discuss any concerns. Holy crap, I sound like an adult!

In what areas of your life could you benefit from setting hours? We can do this together, and together we can reduce the stress of flying by the seat of our pants. After creating your plan using the KISS method (Keep It Simple Sweetie), communicate with those impacted, and let's get started. For twenty-one days, we'll honor ourselves and our supporters by sticking with the hours and journaling about the outcomes. This is a great start for a new, healthy habit.

New Habits

Intention: Determination & focus
Release: Others' energy

I successfully met my new bedtime last night as well as my new wake-up time today. It felt great to enjoy my morning practice and then sit down with coffee and journal in hand. This was followed by the first wrench in my shiny new schedule.

Creating new habits sounds like a perfect solution to all our problems … in the planning stage. We find ourselves upset by the current system. We shift this and stop that, and voilà, we're happy again. But when our seedling habits are disrupted, old habits that we recently found irritating feel easy and familiar, like an old pair of shoes. The temptation is to give up.

But this is where we must support our initial inspiration with determination. This means that when we're derailed, we give ourselves kudos for showing up and starting again. This is how we grow. Fail. Cheer. Start again. Partial fail. Cheer. Start again until our new habit becomes ingrained.

Is there a habit you tried to incorporate into your life but gave up because it just seemed too difficult? Today, write it out in your journal. Make any necessary tweaks using the KISS (Keep It Simple Sweetie) method to set yourself up for success.

People around you may resist the changes you desire in outright or sneaky ways. Don't be deterred. Keep your focus. Embrace the energy of those who support you and release the energy of those who do not. Some may come around over time to cheer you on. But it is *not* your responsibility to absorb the energy of those still resisting.

COLLECTION 5

Navigating

The Search

Intention: Questions & connections
Release: Self-judgment

My son has been sick. The antibiotics he's taking may be addressing the infection, but they're also making him feel very nauseous. Life is already challenging for him, and this just adds to it. I think I should know what to do and always have backup plans B-Z in my back pocket. Yet, I am limited by what I know and what he's willing to do. This doesn't stop the self-criticisms rolling around in my head.

Today, I will renew my trust in the universe that we will make the right connections to meet the right people and access the best resources. Afterall, everything is connected. For my role, I will compile a list of questions and hold space for answers. These answers may come back in the form of more questions, as well as clear solutions. Each will lead us to the next step, the next inquiry, the next hope, and eliminate dead ends. There's no room in this plan for critics—internal or external!

Are you facing something important and puzzling that seems void of solutions? Make a list of questions you have on the topic. Start your search with a quiet meditation to create a space for the right people and resources. And then prepare to receive them. As each idea presents itself, take one step and then the next. Ask plenty of questions, and if your inner critic shows up, invite her to join your quest.

One Task

Intention: Clarity
Release: Blinders & bulls@#t

I sure can waste time! It's amazing how my toenails need to be trimmed, or the garbage taken out when I'm facing a task I don't enjoy.

Rarely do I call myself out on these lame little rabbit trails I follow to avoid, procrastinate, and otherwise leave undone what will have to be done eventually. My behavior can be much like a child who doesn't want to clean her room. Well, the time has come to tap into my inner stern mother, put my hands on my hips, and get down to business!

We do well to see our behaviors for what they are with firmness and compassion. When we've been looking at them for so long with one eye closed, pretending we can't quite tell what's going on, we do ourselves a disservice. Even if it's avoiding the suckiest task ever, it feels great to tackle it head-on and put it behind us. This reduces the underlying stress of the undone task and gives a feeling of accomplishment.

Today, I'm holding myself accountable for completing one thing that I've been putting off. I won't be sidetracked by the cute little squirrel running along the fence rail and will have to live with luke-warm coffee until this task is done. Afterward, I will celebrate with hot coffee and give a big sigh.

Choose one project, chore, or job you have procrastinated. If you prefer to check off a list, grab a piece of paper and write the words TASK LIST and the date. Then, write down the one task you have chosen. Nothing more. Now, roll up your sleeves and knock it out. When you are finished, check that baby off!

Creative Moments

Intention: Creative bubbles
Release: Impossibilities

I've been daydreaming often about uninterrupted time alone, as well as the lack of it.

I continue to work at my new bedtime and wake-up hours, as well as carving out an hour in the morning and one in the afternoon to create. I've encountered some success and a few struggles.

This week, my plan has seemed like an impossibility although I'm not going to give up! I am contemplating how I can take steps toward my goal of having daily, quiet, productive time. As I work toward an entire hour, I have decided that I will ease in with shorter periods of time. Each time I am presented with the opportunity, I will slip into these bubbles regardless of their size. This is a whole new way of working for me because it feels rushed, as if I'm throwing something together haphazardly.

I had this skill down when I was raising children. But in my mid-perimenopausal fifties, it will take all of my focus and plenty of deep breaths to resurrect it. I think I'll keep my phone recording app open for capturing quick ideas and a notebook or two lying around to jot down thoughts. Hmm, maybe it's not as impossible as I thought.

If your current life circumstances make you feel that being productive is impossible, it's time to brainstorm. There's a way that simply has not come across your radar. As Thomas Edison said, "I have not failed. I've just found 10,000 ways that won't work." So, stay open, creative, and curious. Be aware of and slide into those bubbles of time. You will find the path that supplies you with all you need to make impossibilities possible.

Coping

Intention: Peace
Release: Emotional heaviness

At the close of my morning kryas, I chant "shanti" three times. Then I whisper the translation of this beautiful Sanskrit word with my hands at my heart. Peace, peace, peace.

Yesterday, the energy at home was so damned heavy! I kept recalling one of my son's surgeons saying that we would have to be strong to help him transition to life after the accident. At times, I wondered exactly what that would look like and how it would feel like in reality. Other times, mainly on days like yesterday, the words made me angry, and I was more inclined to swear and give the universe two middle fingers! There are other times when I've allowed negative energy to all but consume me until I was depressed.

It's hard enough to help yourself, let alone others, when you feel defeated. This is one of those stretches of life that can either destroy or strengthen. And, either way, it will take its toll.

Today, my intention is peace. I will do my best to seek it, embrace it, be it, and spread it.

When you feel the world weighing you down, please remember that it is temporary. You have everything you need to make it through and be strengthened by this tough patch of life. It may not feel that way now, but it is so. If you need to yell, run, or punch the air, do it. Then, return to the space you created by placing your hands on your heart, saying shanti, shanti, shanti. Peace, peace, peace.

Power Struggle

Intention: Grace
Release: Status quo

Have you gone head-to-head with a three-year-old? When you nudge them toward self-responsibility, it can cause them to dig in their heels and refuse to budge. This happens in adult relationships, too; only time-outs aren't really an option. It's worse with other adults as they have larger bladders, can go longer without food, and can hold on to anger and the will to be right with the most amazing tenacity (like a son-of-a-bitch, as my dad would say).

What was okay last night has become an issue worthy of stonewalling this morning. I'm grateful not to feel confused by our current impasse. I am holding space and have no angst. We can all be fierce about what we want, whether it's independence or dependence. When there is a threat of losing it, we dig in our heels. My personal tendency is toward independence. When I sense a certain level of reliance on someone else, I want to push back. I want to feel more in control. This can create a power struggle.

It's important to have an awareness of our behaviors around dependence and independence—especially in relationships. A worthy goal in our important relationships is to achieve a healthy balance of interdependence. This balance is achieved when each individual provides support and is supported within the relationship and where there is space and grace for personal growth.

If you have a special relationship where you experience regular headlocks, take time to consider whether the struggle stems from a tendency for independence or dependence. Is the status quo keeping you stuck and blocking growth? Journal about your behaviors and how you perceive the other person's behaviors. Maybe it's time for grace.

Communication

Intention: Focused flow
Release: Overthinking

It's Monday again, and I'm ready to tackle my list!

I started having regular hot flashes and night sweats a few weeks ago, and they are affecting my sleep. Thankfully, my motivation is intact this morning. Between navigating my approach to menopause and negotiating my son's own navigation of his permanent injuries, my mind has become a bit of a handful.

I have a reasonable agenda today, most of which I'm looking forward to. After being shut out yesterday, I'm the only one home to help with his daily needs, and I'm not sure if I'm back in his good graces. My sister shared that when she was caring for our mother as she was losing her battle with cancer, she was treated like chopped liver compared to visitors. This is often the case with my son. I find this curious but have decided not to get bogged down in that thought. First, I'll do what I'm not looking forward to, then move to the less mentally and emotionally taxing stuff by maintaining my focus and flow.

It doesn't feel good to be pushed away and seemingly unappreciated, especially when we're putting a great deal of our energy into someone or something. Often though, it's not really about us. Regardless, it's best to address the tension and then let it go. It simply doesn't belong to us, and nothing good will come from overthinking or judging how another processes their pain and grief. We all find our own way through these things. I'll dial into my focus and flow the best I can.

Are you overthinking a situation and not sure how to proceed? Do you feel mistreated by someone your intention is to support, especially as a caregiver? After considering the other person's struggles and your own needs, find an appropriate time for a loving conversation. Then, slip back into your flow.

Space for Creativity

Intention: Creative ideas
Release: Perfection

If I've learned anything in life, it's that creativity and perfection are like oil and water. They simply cannot function in the same space. In fact, perfectionism stunts creativity. This I can attest to personally!

I would qualify myself as a procrastinator, albeit not as much as I have been in the past. What has kept me from starting or completing certain projects or conversations is thinking that they had to be perfect. I've overcome this to a certain extent in the past few years, but this week, I'm slogging along on one project. In my head, ideas spin around, but my inner perfectionist has turned her nose up at each. She's an evil dictator, and I'm left feeling blocked and very uncreative!

I have deadlines, so I've decided to set aside fifteen minutes to brainstorm. Before I start, I take three cleansing breaths (big belly breath in through the nose and sighing it out through an open mouth). Next, I stand in mountain pose with both feet firmly planted for one of the best, quick clearing breaths. As I breathe in through my nose, I stretch my arms above. With a loud, "HA!," I breathe out while lowering my arms and bending over in one rapid movement. I think about filling myself with creative energy through each breath in. With each exhale, I imagine I am pushing out any need for perfection.

Now that there is space, it's time to sit for fifteen minutes, writing down every idea that pops up without reservation.

It's your turn. Try three to five rounds of the breath described above, then let your unfiltered, creative ideas flow.

Stuck Energy

Intention: Take more breaks
Release: Grinding away

Sometimes, I do well at focusing and knocking things out, and other times, it's one squirrel moment after another.

I've committed to a new content creation project for someone that I haven't quite found the rhythm and voice to express. I sat in front of my computer the past two days, trying to give birth to ideas that are not fully formed. I work well by first establishing a theme and then building a series of messages, with each contributing to a greater message. So far, my ideas have been as challenging to capture as … a squirrel?!

Today, I'm not going to chase the quick flashes of inspiration. I'm going to make space for them to come to me by taking periodic breaks to intentionally move out stuck energy. I remind myself that the majority of my best ideas came when I was walking in nature. The current temperature is 12°F with a real feel of -4°F. So, I'll take my movement breaks where I can take in a view of the mass of flakes darting around in the wind through the window. Each time I catch myself grinding away, I'll jump up and move to break up the stagnant and blocked energy. With this plan, I feel excited, hopeful, and ready to focus.

What is your process for creating? How do you break yourself out of the inevitable creative slumps? Have you considered taking more breaks to move? Jump, dance, walk, breathe, flow through some yoga postures, and let your creative juices flow!

Full Breaths

Intention: Awareness of my posture & breath
Release: Holding

It has been frigid, snowing, and blowing for three days. My body feels the effects of each of the multiple times I have bundled up and popped out to shovel for fifteen or twenty minutes. The temperature has been below zero with the windchill and I was mindful of not inhaling the frozen air into my lungs.

When I returned inside and back to my work, I noticed that I continued my shallow breathing. My neck and shoulders were tense as if frozen in place from my response to preserve my heat from the cold wind. It's time to get back to the basics of breathing well! I sit up to lengthen my spine, place my feet on the floor, and fill my lungs completely with my next breath. As I breathe out, I roll my shoulders back and down, and then stretch my neck from side to side. Ahh … I will repeat this many times throughout the day to let go, realign, and reset.

Sometimes, we just forget that we can sit tall and breathe fully. When the blizzards of life dump on us, we often shrink ourselves, keep our eyes down, and shovel until we're worn and barely breathing.

It's okay to come in from the storm, warm up, sit tall, breathe deeply, and take up space. Self-care is even more important when you're up to your neck in alligators. Do your best to relax for now. You'll know when it's time to shovel again, or quite possibly the storm will have passed.

Freedom

Intention: Keep showing up
Release: The unknown

One of the most important things I have learned on my personal healing journey is to simply show up. I have shown up without makeup, without a plan, full of snark, with no bra, feeling like I'm not enough, and when showing up was the last thing I wanted to do. I have shown up in true form and rare form and a hundred other ways. The moments and days have added up to years as I have regularly practiced the habit of showing up as myself.

In the beginning, I was in the habit of hiding—physically and emotionally. I just didn't have the energy to be seen authentically because I lacked self-love, self-acceptance, and self-esteem. I assumed others would see me as I saw myself and that frightened me. What I discovered is that most people struggle in this same way to some degree. Many think that they are just too different and don't fit in anywhere. I used to believe that too. Maybe you think that about yourself.

Although we are each one-of-a-kind, we are all human. Our uniqueness is needed and showing up as ourselves makes the world a better place. Doing so may take the pressure off others grappling to meet an intangible personal or cultural standard as they witness our authenticity.

While you cannot predict how others will perceive you when you shed your mask and step out to be fully seen, you can be confident. No one else can show up as amazingly "you" as you can!

I encourage you to take time to explore the following journaling questions. Do you struggle to be authentic? Do you hold yourself to standards that are completely unreasonable or conflict with your true nature? What would it be like to drop those requirements and simply show up as yourself? If I could choose one word to describe my experience, it would be "freedom."

COLLECTION 6

Changing

Be Spontaneous

Intention: Switch up routine
Release: Agenda

There's something about how an intense winter storm holds us all hostage. Too much time spent inside with dismal and limited natural light, along with the howling winds spinning the snow in all directions, eventually wears down the most committed home-body. It feels great to be cocooned inside where it's warm, shuffling around all day in slippers with a mug of hot coffee in hand—until it doesn't.

There's sunshine hanging around today. Although I'm squinting because it's so bright, it's exactly what I've needed, and it will take the temperature soaring to 20°F. You won't find me working on my computer or doing normal daily tasks inside. My plan is to finish the necessities, bundle up, and head out into the Winter Wonderland with snowshoes strapped on. To hell with the task list and agenda.

When was the last time you stepped out of the same old routine? It doesn't have to be something extreme like buying a ticket on a whim and flying to Mexico (although that sounds amazing right now)! Switching things up is good for our brains, improving cognition. It can generate excitement which is a great treatment for depression, burnout, and cabin fever. Of course, routines are important and necessary and having them makes a periodic deviation very effective.

How will you switch up your day?

You've Come a Long Way

Intention: Ease & soak
Release: Taking things for granted

My snowshoeing jaunt yesterday was wonderful! I can still feel the warmth of the afternoon sun, smell the crisp wintery air, and hear the soft crunch of the snow underfoot. I can also feel my muscles. It was deep, and I had the honor of making the first prints on the blank, white canvas. This takes more effort than following a path. At one point, my step plunged my snowshoe so deep that it took my whole body down, which resulted in some much-needed laughter!

Looking back at my tracks made me feel grateful for how far I've come, and I see what a gift my life experiences have been. The good, the bad, and everything in between. Sometimes, I'm moving too fast and being too busy to really appreciate the moments. I am grateful to soak in this sweet and beautiful reminder.

Have you been missing the moments? It's easy to be swept up and become unaware of life's gifts, especially when the wrapping is ugly. Today, set aside time to soak in the moments. Allow yourself to see how far you have come, all you have made it through, and the many gifts you've received along your path.

Tuning In

Intention: Nurture & nourish
Release: Crud

I am learning to listen to my body.

Yesterday, I felt like I needed to take it easy and limit my time in the freezing weather. Last night, I detected a slight soreness in the back of my throat. This morning, I am obviously sick with some form of winter sinus crud. After a gentle yin practice, I sipped on a cup of hot chicken bone broth and curled up under a blanket. The best thing to do is to nurture and nourish myself.

Until about seven years ago, I was often disconnected from my body and pulsing with anxiety and stress. I pushed myself to the point that I had an energetic crash in my 40s. That experience slowed me down, but I still had much to learn about tuning in and caring for my sweet self. That's when I tried yoga. Not only my body, but my mind and emotions soaked up the holistic nurturing. I knew I had found a practice that was healing and nourishing to my entire being, including my body.

What is your relationship to your body? Do you listen to her when she is seeking your attention? Do you care for her when she is sick? Having practices that build and support the mind-body connection is extremely important.

Yoga offers a wide range of therapy for your mind, body, emotions, and spirit through all life experiences and seasons. Starting today, incorporate at least five minutes of any yogic practice. This includes breath, chanting, meditation, and/or postures that involve movement or stillness. Listen to your body and choose something that feels nurturing and nourishing.

Home

Intention: Nurture & nourish
Release: Resistance

Although I'm feeling much better today, I'm not 100 percent. Right now, I'm basking in an hour alone at home which is a complete anomaly compared to two years ago.

I lived by myself in this very home then. After raising four children as a widowed single parent, living alone felt like a sweet reward to enjoy this space that was witness to all the memory-making over the years. Those feelings of having space to myself, to just be, have come back to me this afternoon. Both thoughts of a full house and those of me shuffling around doing "Kathy things" (my son's description of my meanderings) warm my heart.

Life is different now, or is it? In reality, the cycle has come back around to a full house. As such, I long for undisturbed time to shuffle around, or more likely shuffle off for yet another pee break, a generous reward for being a member of the 50s club. I recognize and honor this natural cycle of expansion and contraction. Regardless of how full or empty, this home is still a place of love and safety. For that, I'm grateful.

Today, I will allow myself to be nourished and nurtured by "home." I will surrender any resistance to my current season of life and be present to make more memories on which to reflect when I find myself alone again.

Do you have a full house, or are you living alone? How would you describe the season of life you are in? Are you resisting or embracing it? Consider if you are currently in a state of expansion or contraction. Your home is or should be your safe space. It should feel nourishing and nurturing whether you're shuffling around in slippers alone or it is filled to the brim.

Honoring Change

Intention: Do something to honor Winter Solstice
Release: Darker days

It's officially the first day of winter and the day with the fewest daylight hours of the year. That also means it will be the longest night.

In our little corner of the world, the sunrise was at 7:30 a.m. and will set in the frozen sky by 4:21 a.m. The temperature started at -10°F and will continue dropping to tonight's low of -30°F. Tomorrow, the temps will be much the same. On the day of the Winter Solstice, we are tilted as far away from the sun as possible, which means that the sun's path across the southern sky is as low as it can be.

This is the season and weather that has taken me to dark places in the past. The freezing temperatures keep me inside, and the limited daylight makes me feel lethargic. Both are opposites to my internal wiring. I love being outdoors, and I'm very active. This year, I'm doing well, thankfully. But I'd like to honor this special day as a way to release the darker days and welcome the start of a brighter future.

I will set aside time this evening for a candlelight meditation. The candle will represent the sun's gradual return to its place higher in the sky, making the days longer. It will be a celebration of joyful days ahead and the manifestation of dreams.

Join me in a candlelight meditation or choose another ritual to honor and celebrate Winter Solstice. Take time to welcome the longer, brighter days and months ahead, and release the darker days.

Blocks

Intention: Trust myself
Release: Holding back

Being a recovering perfectionist means that I'm also a procrastinator, which gets not just one but two sucks!

I'm going to spend a few of these last days of the year focusing on trusting myself. I would like to cut down on the time it takes me to create and finish projects…and walk away feeling satisfied with my work.

Trust is a core value for me, and self-trust is essential to living fully. A lack thereof stifles creativity and expression, both of which I currently find myself struggling to free. I'm going to spend time sitting with, feeling into, and moving through these blocks. I'm too much in my head and missing the authentic way I have created and worked from my heart in the past.

Let's go on this journey together. Today, decide on one aspect of you that is blocked (e.g., creativity, intimacy, generosity). Next, we'll both write down how being stuck in this area is impacting life. Meet me tomorrow for the next step.

Clearing

Intention: Trust myself
Release: Holding back

Now that we have pinpointed our respective areas where we are blocked and have written down how it is affecting our lives, it's time to sit with, feel into, and begin moving through the blocked energy. This may take a day, a week, or longer. But our focus will draw energy in to nurture self-trust, and the change we want will come in its time if we stick with it.

I've begun to use my meditation time to sit with my creativity blocks. It's uncomfortable. As emotions surface, an inner voice starts to make excuses for why I cannot create. More discomfort. I feel defeated, then distracted, and finally I'm aware that something has shifted. It's a slight shift, but there is movement, nonetheless. This affirmation comes to mind: It is easy for me to be in the free flow of creativity.

I will use this statement to continue my exploration and to dissolve my fears about writing and speaking from my heart. There is work to be done, and I am grateful that I have started.

Make a commitment to spend at least five minutes each day this week to take your area of focus into meditation. Quiet and stillness may invite discomfort, but please sit with this feeling. It will pass. You will not only be clearing blocks, but you will also be teaching yourself an essential tool for life. The clearing may need more than one week, so be patient, trust the process, and trust yourself. I assure you the shift is happening.

Day Off

Intention: Slow down to rest & read
Release: Guilt

I did not take it easy yesterday. In fact, I overdid it!

I'm tired, but motivated. This is a combination I often experience, and after a couple cups of coffee, I usually forget that I need a down day. With a full practice under my belt and two cups of half-caf hitting my nervous system, I'm raring to take on the day. Plan A is in effect, and it's time to hit the gas! Well, maybe …

Thankfully, my sweet inner voice has given me the green light to sit on the couch, journal, write, and read with my feet up. The older I get, the less I feel guilty about laying around. Yet, I do feel a little bad for not planning anything today. We don't really celebrate Christmas, but we usually gather for dinner, family time, and maybe some simple gift giving. Today … nothing. Goodbye, guilt, and hello plan B.

Do you need a real day off and not just a day off from what you are paid to do? We all need time to rejuvenate our minds and bodies. And, since no one else knows exactly what we need, it's up to us to create and tap into plan B. Christmas is a great time to take advantage of the seasonal slowdown. With many stores closed and people staying home, why not give yourself a guilt-free rest day?

Small Shifts

Intention: Self-awareness
Release: Expectations

Damn, I had the most amazing snowshoeing experience yesterday!

I weaved around in the forest, sometimes on a path, and other times I blazed my own. The sun was bright, the sky blue, and the clouds were swept across the heavens in the powerful wind. I felt exuberant to be out among the trees! Surrounded, I felt protected and free as I soaked in the freshness and beauty of the winter forest.

My intention yesterday was to slow down, and aside from snowshoeing, I did. But being in nature is therapy for me. My body is tired today, so I spent much of my practice breathing into spots of tension and tightness. I've been going to bed and waking earlier to give myself more time to rest and to enjoy my morning yoga practice. I'm noticing how much more peaceful I feel afterward. I'm more prepared for the morning routine with my son and ready to tackle a few key tasks during the day. I am also experiencing less stress when my expectations are sideswiped.

Small shifts can lead to big changes and small shifts are easier to manage. Intention setting is one way to take small, focused steps toward reshaping your life if that is your desire. And there are wonderful unintended outcomes, too. Don't miss them by being too attached to preconceived expectations.

Use the following questions as a simple practice to open up to self-awareness. Is today's intention applicable to you? Do you need to reword it or choose one that suits you better? Ponder these questions and align yourself with YOUR intention.

It's Natural

Intention: Embrace the natural ebb & flow of energies
Release: Fear

I'm excited to feel myself drawn back into a creative flow of energy. I rely on, and others rely on, my intuitive nature and authentic approach to writing and teaching. When that energy is ebbing, it scares me.

There is a natural ebb and flow to all of life, but it's hard for me to remember and accept this when it feels like I've rolled from the mountain top down into the valley. Each time I experience this cycle, it takes me less time to look around the valley to see what I can learn. Sometimes, it gives me the opportunity for much needed rest—unless I fight it! In that case, I spend as much time as it takes stressing myself out. In the end, I realize my predicament and release the fear (either willingly or because I'm exhausted). Then comes surrender. I rest until I feel the familiar energetic tug once again.

It's okay to feel uncreative and/or unproductive. Embrace it. It's part of the natural cycle of life, and when you are ebbing, give yourself a break. Literally, show yourself kindness and compassion, and release any fear. Nourish and nurture your mind, body, and soul. Go within and rest. Soon, you will be drawn back into the flow.

COLLECTION 7

Trusting

You Can Get It

Intention: Satisfaction
Release: Judgment

I feel a good deal of satisfaction from a job well done. But I don't easily give myself credit, kudos, or even a stoic, approving nod. It's something I often gloss over, thinking that there are plenty of others that could have done just as well or maybe better.

Today, I'm going to be aware of each accomplishment and pause to breathe and soak in the satisfaction of a job done well—no matter how small. The alarm went off at 6 am, and I was on the mat by 6:30 am to get my day started. Satisfied! The kitchen faucet has an irreparable leak. I researched a replacement that is quality, fits the space, and is within budget. Satisfied! I painlessly created media for myself and for a client for the next two days. Mmmm … very satisfying! It sure feels great to give myself credit. These positive vibes leave no room for judgment.

How about we both prove Mick (Jagger) wrong with a "CAN" attitude and squeeze some satisfaction out of this day?! Yeah!

Unrestricted

Intention: Move freely
Release: Lack

Yesterday was a blur and … only semi-satisfying. There, I said it!!

Wait a minute. Even though I've been critical, I still see that I made progress, so I have to admit that it was actually rather satisfying.

Today is Friday, and I am switching up my day. We've been building a house in the midst of the aftermath of the chaos of my son's car crash six months ago. I'm going to pick out kitchen cabinets and countertops and gather more information to settle on the layout. I get to build a color board to help wrap my head around a cohesive theme throughout the kitchen and house. Fun! I'm also going to take extra time away to do my daily writing in a coffee shop where I won't be on call. I'm excited for the opportunity to move freely—mentally, physically, emotionally, and spiritually.

You've probably surmised that I don't get out much these days, and you're right. I had been left to my own devices as an active fifty-some-year-old, single, empty-nester up until about two years ago. Now, I feel limited when it comes to getting out and about. My partner and I had been filling our days and weeks traveling, hiking, biking, and working. It felt like freedom. But I haven't quite figured out what freedom looks and feels like in my current circumstances.

Is there a part of your life where you feel bound up? Are you going through a season that feels like lack? Give yourself a day or an hour to move freely. This will remind you of what is always available. It's usually our thinking that makes us feel restricted. I encourage you to use this reminder to be free in your mind until your next physical outing.

Vision

Intention: Review, reflect, release, revision
Release: Self-limitations

Man, I love the excitement of closing one year and stepping into the next! Just as each morning gives the gift of a fresh start, the new year offers this gift but in a much larger package.

I also enjoy how creating a vision board provides a tactile way to begin with a fresh canvas and to creatively answer some very important questions. What do I really want? Where do I see myself going? What do I want to do? What have I already started that I want to carry into the new year? What is best left behind? How can I live more aligned with my values? Which behaviors should I keep and which should I release? What do I want to learn?

All of these questions, but not nearly as many answers. Before me are twelve months, fifty-two weeks, and 365 days, just like last year. Today, I'll spend time reviewing and reflecting. I'll give myself time and space to take a walk back through the year, journaling as I make my way through the months, weeks, and days. I've experienced joy, tragedy, laughs, grief, and much I did not plan or expect. As always, the year ahead will have more new experiences to offer.

My visioning practice is a way to send the energy of intention out before me. It helps me find clarity and to align my thoughts and actions. It's a grand, affirming gesture and request to the universe that I'm present and holding space in my heart and life to make my dreams a reality.

Starting today, take time over the next week to review and reflect on the past year. Then, release what no longer serves you or has run its course. Next, it's time to dream into the year ahead by creating a vision board. You may want to use poster boards, magazines, stickers, markers, and other tools to craft your vision. Approach the activity with the mindset that anything is possible! No censoring! You may even want to gather friends and family together for a visioning get-together. Have fun dreaming!

P.S. A vision board isn't exclusively for the new year. Consider creating one for a new chapter or new beginning. You may want to look into making an online vision board as an alternative.

Out with the Old

Intention: Visioning the year
Release: Past & future

It's time! Time to let the past be a memory. Time to dream and float the intentions for a new chapter, a new beginning, and a new year out into the universe.

To me, intentions are a vital part of creating the life I want. They are the energy of what I desire. What I desire now is based on my present understanding of who I am and why I'm here. I used to be confused about why I was unable to manifest my every intention. I've come to see that they are an ideal that I grow toward. The magic is not only in reaching my goal but even more so in all of the delightful, heartbreaking, and uneventful experiences along the way. Often, what I was sure I wanted when I set my intention is transformed by the magic of the journey.

Today, I express my gratitude for the past year before gently tucking it away in my memory chest. It's time to create a vision for the year ahead, to gather my intentions and release them like leaves in the autumn breeze. Let the journey continue!

It's difficult to bring in the new when the old is taking up too much space. Allow your past to retire into memories, use your present to hold space, and allow your intentions to create your future.

What's Your Plan

Intention: Efficiency
Release: Force

I think the word "efficiency" sounds like a business term, but I'm making it my intention anyway. Having grown up in, worked in, and operated family businesses (and now my own), I think quite a lot about how to organize and reorganize space and processes to be as productive as possible with the least waste. I admit that I do like a good plan!

When my kids were teenagers, I often asked them, "What's your plan?" Now, I'm asking myself that question. In my experience of taking a willy-nilly approach to a project or day, I'm not all that productive, yet somehow, I've worn myself out. This is another reason that I love setting intentions. Today, I will be mindful of how I move and how I arrange what I want to carry out, but not in a bullwhip, taskmaster sort of way. Efficiency is a continuous process of adjustments and tweaks until there is a smooth flow. Being forceful with myself is a sure way to lose the focus and balance I'm enjoying this morning.

Are there areas of your life that are unproductive and wearing you out? Would a few switch-ups reduce the amount of energy needed to reach your goal? Choose one area and make some thoughtful adjustments. Before you know it, you'll have a smooth, efficient flow, resulting in more production and ease.

Jump

Intention: Timing
Release: Reacting to triggers

Timing is everything—as the saying goes.

It's important to know when the timing is right … even though it may not always feel quite right. Being uncomfortable is okay. Squirming a little bit is healthy. Being nudged to move forward is helpful when I'm dragging my feet.

The times in my life when I have put myself out there and jumped in when I was afraid are some of the most exhilarating and memorable. But when I'm prodded by someone else, I can feel triggered. This is what I experienced last night and this morning. My immediate response was to push back by making an excuse. I really had to acknowledge and shut down the fiery little lady inside with her hands on her hips saying, "I'll do it when I'm damned good and ready!" It makes me smile and shake my head as I reflect on her sassy disposition. But she's wrong to fight this nudge. We both know the timing is right.

I decided to embrace the nudge and get moving! And it felt great to jump in. I'm thankful for my fiery protector, although she can easily become overly protective, leaving me stuck as a victim of my fears. The last thing I want is to be controlled by fear. Taking a closer look at my triggers has given me opportunities for growth by getting to know myself better. I'm grateful for friends who care enough to give me a gentle push when needed, and also for the will to nudge myself.

Consider what you are missing by giving in to your fear triggers. There is no space in this activity for judgment. We all recoil and play the victim at times because it has served us at some point. Pay attention to which triggers hold you back and which triggers actually protect you. Step out from behind your protector's shadow when you feel in your gut that it's time to jump in as scary as it may be. Opportunities are about timing. Be uncomfortable. Squirm. And do it anyway.

AAA Approach

Intention: Overcoming
Release: Timing

Yesterday's intention is today's release.

I trust that the time will come when life won't be so damned challenging, and until then, I'll face all the small and daunting obstacles as they come.

For me, overcoming is a continuous process because life regularly throws curveballs. And how irritating that I don't get to choose the timing and duration! My best tactics to date are awareness, acknowledgement, and acceptance. This AAA approach is what I also practice during meditation when my mind wanders.

Having awareness is a habit that I have developed to deal with anxiety. By paying attention to and engaging in the present moment, I reduce the distraction of past experiences and the lure of future predictions. When shit pops up, I'm on top of it and seeing it for what it is in the moment. If it's highly unpleasant, I acknowledge that aspect with something like, "This really hurts!" or "This sucks!" The final A can take more effort and time, but it's the step forward that leads to growth. Acceptance of something that hurts and pushes me past what I thought I could handle reminds me that I have far more potential than I know. By accepting hardship, I don't necessarily agree with or appreciate the experience. It means that I accept how things are. When that happens, I have changed my mindset from victim to problem solver.

I encourage you to use the 3 A's for your next challenge. Until then, practice this approach in daily meditation. Meditation is not about emptying your mind, which I believe may be possible for a monk in a cave, but it's a rarity for those of us in the trenches.

Here's how to practice the AAA's in meditation. Choose a focus (maybe your heart space). This becomes the center of your awareness as you breathe in and out of this space. When (not if) you become aware that your mind is no longer focused on that space, you acknowledge the wandering, accept that your mind has drifted, and return to your heart focus. This process may repeat many times during even a five-minute meditation. If that's your experience, you are normal. The AAA meditation is an excellent practice for the real-life version of overcoming.

Investing

Intention: Trusting in & awareness of support
Release: Inauthenticity

There have been blips in life where I have not felt supported, but overall, my experience has been one of all things working together to buoy me up.

At times, I have been stuck in negative mental loops and became depressed, even suicidal. Once I let myself slip so far, I was left with someone I didn't trust, someone who was disconnected and draining. *Me!* I felt like a cloud of anxious, hopeless thoughts.

When my children were young, I would help them clean their rooms. The rule was that I would put as much energy into it as they did. If they dinked around, I would no longer help. I have learned that the universe operates much the same. In my darkest times, when I barely put energy into myself, I felt alone and without purpose. If I put even an ounce of effort into pulling out of a slump, that effort was matched. My investment in myself could not and cannot be faked. Dinking around (a.k.a., being inauthentic) does not produce results. What I put in is magically and loyally matched. Zero effort yields nothing.

Tonight, there is a full moon. A full moon is about completion, meaning it is a perfect time to release and remove what is no longer working, is complete, or has run its course. My focus will be to let go of any of the fake, half-assed attempts at creating the life that I want. As I put forth true effort and heartfelt energy, I will trust and watch as the universe generates and provides an equal amount of magic.

Do you feel supported in life? In what ways do you contribute your part so the universe can do its part? Is there something, just one thing, you can do right now to invest in yourself? Depending on where you are in life currently, this could be anything from taking a nap to exercising to forgiveness. Take fifteen to twenty minutes to write in your journal about how you will do your part, then roll up your sleeves and get started.

Acceptance

Intention: Do my best
Release: Clinging to what is lost

To be honest, I feel some sadness today.

When my partner came home from playing music at a local restaurant, he shared his joy in creating and blending with other musicians. We used to do this together. We were invited to visit my brother in Florida in February, but that isn't realistic at this point either. It hit me sideways that I had lost much in the chaos of the crash and life thereafter. It feels a lot like grief.

One of the Four Agreements in Don Miguel Ruiz's book of the same name is to always do your best. Today, that's my intention. I'm going to give myself a little time and space to grieve the loss of the life I had. Life has changed drastically, and my day-to-day looks much different than I planned. I no longer feel free, spontaneous, and energized like I did before. I've worked my way through awareness, acknowledgement, and acceptance several times, but it looks like I'll be going through the process again. I'll do it as many times as it takes until I am able to let go of what is lost.

Awareness, acknowledgment, and acceptance make up the AAA's. This process sets us up on the path of forward movement and growth. There is much in life we cannot control, but the AAA's allow us to do things on our own terms regardless, which is very empowering. Because after we find acceptance, we open the door to creating a new life and exploring new possibilities.

Join me today by simply doing your best. Apply the AAA process by first noticing what you are clinging to that has been lost, affirming that the loss is disrupting your peace, and accepting it for what it is. Allow your emotions to flow and move through. You will know when you reach acceptance.

Open

Intention: See possibilities
Release: Limiting thoughts

When I awoke this morning, I shuffled out to the kitchen to turn on the electric kettle. As I looked up from the sink, I saw the moon hovering, lit up in pink from the sunrise, as she made her final appearance before slipping out of sight. I thought of the full moon intention I made just two days ago and felt affirmed, acknowledged, and supported.

I used to be more of a realist, but these days, I leave plenty of space for the miraculous and unexpected. This does not keep me from dealing with life situations head-on. But it does change how I think about and perceive them. It's important for me to see things as they are, and equally important to envision them as they could be. Some call it dreaming. It boils down to having an awareness that possibilities in life are vast. This cannot happen with a closed mind and limited thinking. Like anything, we have to believe first.

Most grand dreams seem impossible. In my experience, those are the best ones! Today, I encourage you to allow yourself space to be a dreamer and visionary. If you don't have a list of dreams and desires, gift yourself time, paper and pen, and free range for your heart and mind to explore without reservation. No limits! Your inner belief and openness will allow you to see the possibilities clearly.

COLLECTION 8

Appreciating

Simply Trust

Intention: Small changes
Release: Results

I woke up feeling somewhat irritable.

Even yesterday, I was not looking forward to Monday, which is unusual for me. There is nothing to dread, yet I feel something is off. Each morning, I take whatever energy I'm feeling to my mat and sort it out. But today, I can't shake the sense that something is out of balance.

Over the years, I've learned to pay attention and trust my gut when there's a blip on my radar. Experience has taught me to listen. There have been too many instances where I have discounted such messages. Later, I would understand the meaning and wished I had responded. In the beginning, I would heed the subtle prods of small things like the urge to double-check that I locked the door or slow down while driving. When these actions proved beneficial—and saved me from potential problems or harm, I leveled up my trust in bigger things. Of course, there were plenty of times that it seemed like the feeling led to nothing, as far as I could tell.

In the process of learning to trust my intuition, I learned to appreciate being connected in mind, body, and soul. This is the overarching reason that I love yoga so much. By knowing how it feels to be connected and in balance, it's easy to sense the opposite.

Intuition is an innate gift that everyone possesses but not all utilize. The first step to tapping into this gift is making practices that help you connect your mind, body, and spirit a daily priority. Yoga in all of its forms is perfect. Breathwork, meditation, chanting, and mindful movement train your brain to pay attention. Consistent yoga practice is a tool to gather all your scattered pieces into one beautiful, harmonious whole. It teaches you what it feels like to be present and balanced. It prepares you for life off the mat by tuning you into all of your senses and awakening your intuition.

Today is a great day to make a small change by paying more attention and listening more intently. As you respond to this superpower—your intuition—don't worry about the results. Simply trust.

Balance

Intention: Slow & steady
Release: Intensity

Yesterday's schedule was blown up. But today, I'm clicking along fearlessly. Whatever time I have to myself to get things done will be slow and steady. No rushing. No running. My pace today is measured … so far.

I'm not sure if you ever do this, but I start some days like I'm launching out of the blocks for the 100-meter dash. That's not necessarily a bad thing, right?! Some projects require high energy and speed. But for the marathon of life, a reasonable pace will get us all the way to the finish line without having to crawl along half alive. Either way, no matter the distance, we must condition ourselves for the short and long journey of life. To do this, we need to understand when to sprint and when to proceed slowly and steadily. Life is about seeking balance.

Today, choose the intention and release you need most. Slow and steady or fast and furious? Check-in with yourself and decide if you need the intensity to sprint or if a marathon pace suits you better. Place both palms over your heart and sit still and quiet for one to five minutes. Breathe full belly breaths and allow yourself to tune in to what your heart needs most.

Opportunities

Intention: Appreciation
Release: Overwhelm

It seems like I have too many plates spinning in the air. But I'm proud of myself for getting organized and not overthinking every little detail. If I've learned anything over the past year, it is to live in the present moment, moving one step at a time—especially when life is spilling over.

I scheduled an appointment for next month, then realized that I had other obligations that day already. It seemed like light years away when I made those commitments, and now they are right around the corner. This prompted me to look at my calendar for the entire year. Interesting and enlightening! It's like someone else was looking out for me and had a good deal of faith that I could manage. On one hand, I'm a little overwhelmed. On the other hand, I'm grateful for the opportunities my last year's self has lined up for me.

Have you experienced the sensation of tension creeping into your body when you have a lot on your plate? What if you paused to compile a list of appreciation? Any day is the perfect day to appreciate having so much to look forward to … new experiences, creations, collaborations, and fertile soil for growth. When you finish your list, step into your day with full awareness, confidence, and gratitude for the amazing opportunities before you.

Sensitivity

Intention: Encouragement
Release: Fear of outcome

There are times when someone close to me is struggling and I'm not sure what to say. Possible words to comfort them come to mind, only to be dismissed by a critical inner voice. On some occasions, when I do say them, they are rejected or resisted. I get it. We all need space to process. Ultimately, using sensitivity to encourage others when they have hit a snag in life is a great approach.

When I am given encouragement from friends or family, it sticks with me even if I'm not ready to hear it at the time, and even if they stumble on their words. I still feel supported. I still feel loved. It's their genuine intention to show love and support, not just their words.

When you have loved ones that seem resistant to your support, give it to them anyway. Override the inner judge and the fear of being rejected. Let love ring out through your encouragement.

One of the best ways to put this into practice is with oneself. Try speaking to yourself using words that uplift and inspire. This can become a wonderful habit!

Be Hopeful

Intention: Optimism
Release: Doubtful thoughts

It's Friday, and aside from the regular responsibilities, I don't have anything planned until late in the afternoon. Thinking about this makes me feel free, at ease, and exceptionally optimistic.

For me, being optimistic is a balance between accepting what is and imagining what can be. By definition, being optimistic is to be hopeful and expectant for the future. When I am willing to see past obstacles and/or recognize they may hold lessons and solutions needed to manifest my dreams, I come closer to connecting what is to what is possible. This intoxicating energy leaves little space for old, doubtful thoughts.

Realistically, we can be optimistic every day. It's a choice and a perspective that is always available. Am I always optimistic? Absolutely not! But I'm doing the work each day to replace past, unhelpful ways of thinking (that got me nowhere or worse) with practices that support progressive growth. The mind is extraordinarily powerful whether we use it to be doubtful or hopeful. So why not be optimistic?

Waste Not

Intention: Don't waste a good crisis
Release: Aftermath emotions & thinking

Winston Churchill stated, "Never let a good crisis go to waste." Yesterday, my son and I experienced a "good crisis" in our home. Now I'm contemplating how to use it for good.

It feels unnatural to string the words "good" and "crisis" together. Mostly, we seek to avoid emotions coming to an explosive head and filling the air with intensity. That level of energy has a way of sticking around in the body as tension, and the mind as spinning thoughts, and powerful emotions. It stresses every part of our being.

In my recent experience, I was grateful for my grounded responses that kept me from being swept up in the whirlwind. But afterward, I set a personal record time on my walk up the mountain! It helped me to move the crazy energy and do some mental sorting. Before bed, I'd felt angry. This morning, I know it's time to make changes in this relationship.

The conversation I'm anticipating is open and honest. I'm actually looking forward to establishing new boundaries and more clarity of expectations *for both of us*. While this dramatic outburst triggered me, it felt empowering to choose my response. It revealed personal growth as well as where I have work to do. All in all, I think that I've released remnants of the aftermath and avoided wasting a good crisis.

It's likely that you have been subjected to someone's emotional crisis. Recall a specific incident. How did you respond (no judgment!)? Can you put your finger on how you were triggered regardless of whether you reacted externally? As you reflect back, consider what good could come from the experience. Record your thoughts in your journal.

Moments

Intention: Enjoy
Release: All that impedes abundance

I've decided to take my daily intentions back to the basics: Optimism, appreciation, overcoming, doing my best, seeing possibilities, encouragement, and other topics. Today, I intend to experience joy in the exciting and in the mundane, and let this desire cover the undesirable.

Engaging in the present opens me up to the full, front-row experience of each moment. There will never be another moment exactly like the present. This reminds me of a kind and passionate southern gentleman pastor at a church I went to years ago who would express this each Sunday. He'd say, "We'll never be gathered here quite like this again." It's true. Nothing stays the same. My days are not on repeat, even when I feel like Bill Murray in *Groundhog Day*. When I feel excited, it's only exciting compared to previous experiences.

The new and unknown that each day brings is most often accompanied by some of the same old stuff. But the old stuff is valuable because its familiarity is comfortable. For this same reason, it can easily be taken for granted if we don't pay attention. And, if we're not mindful, we might just go through the motions and let the abundance of the moments slip away unacknowledged.

It's a great day to be tuned in. It's a great day to breathe in joy and breathe out busy thoughts. Each moment is filled with the gift of abundance. Let's examine and savor each one.

Peripheral Vision

Intention: Focused but open
Release: Trying too hard

I was up early this morning and soaked in a peaceful practice. Everything is gliding along beautifully, and I am grateful for the quiet time to write and be creative. I feel supported by nature as I watch the snow fall gently, slowly adding to the layers lining each bare branch and every other surface. I feel deep gratitude.

It's Monday, and I'm looking forward to tackling a few adulting tasks, such as paying bills and preparing for clients. I find it easy to dive in and go like hell, but that technique doesn't work for this new phase of life. And honestly, it may never have worked very well. I can become so fixed on my agenda that I am oblivious to the glitter of abundance floating around me. This also happens when I push too hard. Things are challenging for a reason. Sometimes, it's a nudge to support growth, and other times, there's simply a better way.

Today, expand your field of vision to include the universe's often subtle sparkles. Just as you are aware of falling snow, rain, or other subtle movements in your peripheral, allow yourself to be aware and open to other ways and opportunities.

Pause First

Intention: Breathe!
Release: Tension

We have a saying in our family: Give her the onion!! It means to crank down and stomp on the gas pedal as more power is needed.

My sleepy, quiet morning has gone rogue. The plan for building an in-house support system to help care for my son must begin anew. We were informed that in thirty days we will no longer have our current service. Both of our amazing helpers were here at the same time this morning due to a schedule change. I managed to squeeze in four of several phone calls on my list to keep things moving forward before their arrival. I'm back at my desk to start where I left off … again. I have an hour to GSD before getting my son moving toward the door so we can (hopefully) get to physical therapy on time. It's an event! Then, we'll be back home to get him settled in and prepare a meal.

I've managed to schedule appointments every day this week which is causing me to feel stressed. That is my cue to pause, breathe, and let the tension pour out. When I have reset and grounded my energy? It's time to "give her the onion!"

Do you have more on your schedule than you would like? Can you feel your shoulders creeping up toward your ears? Pause in stillness with both feet firmly on the ground. Close your eyes. Breathe fully. Imagine physical, mental, and emotional tension pouring out with each exhale. When you sense a calm, groundedness, you are ready to get back to work—or give her the onion. I recommend repeating this process often!

Progress

Intention: Self-care
Release: Worry

I'm working through some misalignment in my back and neck. Over the past couple of weeks, I've been experiencing a decent level of discomfort. If you're someone who visits a chiropractor regularly, you know the drill: Get adjusted. Ice. Feel relief. Ice. Heal. Live life. Feel pain/discomfort again. Get adjusted. Ice. More healing. Feel relief, etc.

This process is not unlike life. It starts when we feel pain or discomfort. This may cause us to reach out for support and take better care of ourselves. As a result, we begin to heal and really live life again. Inevitably, a tinge of pain surfaces once again, and the entire process repeats. Of course, it only repeats in full when we make the choice to get the support we need and make self-care a priority.

Healing takes time, and it may seem like that step never really happens. Just as my regular visits to the chiropractor realign my spine and put my body in a place to heal, I have to do my part … and be patient. Healing from emotional injury can also take time. In my experience, there is no defining moment when I can shout, "I'm healed!" Especially for the major hits! It's more of an awareness that the emotions that once felt overpowering are no longer present in a way that causes pain. This lessening is a sign of healing. So, I'm not going to worry because I'm making progress.

I won't even ask if you have experienced pain or discomfort in your body and/or mind. I'm going to assume that you would answer yes. In which case, I encourage you to get the support you need. Make your self-care the highest priority. Hold space for your healing. Acknowledge your progress. When a dull ache is felt again, don't worry or be discouraged; just repeat the process.

COLLECTION 9

Acknowledging

Risk

Intention: Stay in the opening
Release: Fear

I feel the forward momentum of energy around and within me. I feel the urge to dive in completely and ride the wave. Afterall, taking risks is at the core of growth and is an action that keeps life exciting.

I'm sure I have let many opportunities slip by throughout my life because I was afraid. I don't know if it's age or learning to trust myself (likely both), but it seems easier to dive in these days. And when the universe is lifting me up and revealing some cool shit, I'm all ears.

Being in an opening is all about actively stepping into the unknown. It's about awareness, too. It's never wise to jump into something willy-nilly and without regard for the risks. Being cognizant of potential consequences and unknowns, accepting their possibilities, and then going forward anyway gets the heart pounding in the most wonderful way. Fear is a factor but not a deal breaker. There is risk involved with playing it too safe, and that is a passive choice. It's also boring and difficult to grow on the sidelines of life.

Think of a time when you allowed fear to hold you back from an opportunity. Would you respond differently today? Why or why not? Record your thoughts in your journal.

Resolution

Intention: Clear up loose ends
Release: What is no longer relevant

Having bits and pieces of projects or conversations dangling here and there feels unsettling to me. Whatever the reason for something being undone, it's still undone and simmering on the back burner of my mind.

Movies that leave me hanging and responsible for making up an ending are not my favorite. I have so many questions afterward. I spend far too much time ruminating on what could have happened to the characters. Why not just provide a nice, tidy finish? It's a movie! Make it happen! Of course, real life is something altogether different. I don't get to hand all the characters in my life a script that they follow to wrap everything up to make me feel better. There are always loose ends.

Sometimes we get the opportunity to complete all the details of a project or find closure to a conversation or relationship. Other times, we are left to live without resolution. We can be courageous and compassionate in our approach to situations or people that present us with an opportunity to work out our own ending. It might not be how we want the story to end, but that's okay. We can only do our best. Some fragments may never be resolved. Some we let go, but for others it may be too late or completely out of our control. Then what? Are we left spinning for eternity?

If you feel you have unfinished business with something or someone with no chance of addressing things directly, I have a couple of suggestions. The first is journaling. Write out what you would have done or said. Lay it all out without reservation. The second is specifically applicable to finding closure for a relationship. Place two chairs so they are facing each other. One chair is for you. The other is the person you want to express yourself to. You can also place a representative in this chair—a friend, plant, or stuffed animal. When you're settled, have the conversation. Lay it all out and say what you need to say. It may feel awkward, even silly, but it's effective.

Today, take time to tie up a loose end or two. You deserve the peace.

Ideal Day

Intention: Take the day off
Release: The urge to work

As I journaled this morning, I realized that I have not had a day off in a very long time. By my definition, a day off is when I don't do all the same things I do on the days that I work.

To be transparent with myself, I admit there are a couple of responsibilities for my business that I need to knock out, after which I'll begin my day off. I've already enjoyed a hot bath this morning while sipping on my first cup of hot, creamy coffee. I'd say I'm off to a good start! Of course, there are tasks as a caregiver that I cannot neglect, but aside from that, I'm going to resist any urge to work. A perfect day off for me includes something outdoors and movement. It's winter, so hiking or snowshoeing will be on the agenda. At some point, I'm going to lounge on the couch with a book, an activity that is far too rare.

When was the last time you took a day off, leaving any work safely tucked away? Think about your ideal day in detail. Write about it in your journal, then schedule it on your calendar.

Hold Space

Intention: Balance others' autonomy with needed intervention
Release: Overriding

As a parent of adult children, I often find myself at a fork in the road: Keep my mouth closed and allow them to have their own experience, or offer alternative ways of seeing a situation and other choices available.

I have some very strong-willed children! (Geez, I wonder how that happened?!) Sometimes, they ask for advice, and other times they don't. This is perfect. But when I see them moving toward danger, I feel inclined to intervene. Even in serious circumstances, the choice ultimately belongs to them.

My approach is to start a conversation and ask questions, so I understand their reasoning. Then I ask more questions based on their answers. This helps them move through a process of seeing the situation more clearly, including potential consequences. It may be that they choose a different path after we talk. It may also be that they hold fast to their initial decision. Regardless of whether I agree or disagree, I must honor their free will to choose for themselves. If I see a train wreck, heartache, or major setbacks awaiting, then I can ask to share my perspective and hold space and honor their autonomy.

I've had some wonderful people in my life who have helped me walk through difficult decisions. I have a special appreciation and respect for those brave enough to have a conversation and secure enough not to force their opinion. As I do my best to practice what they taught me, I realize that there are consequences to "letting" people I love make decisions I believe are harmful. This hits me right in the gut. It's a hard thing to do. This makes me even more grateful for my mentors and teachers who held space for me.

Try to recall two experiences: One where you were respected to make your own decision and the second where someone overrode you, dishonoring your autonomy. Record your recollections in your journal, making sure to include how you felt.

It Will Pass

Intention: Awareness
Release: Heaviness

If I were to step on the scale this morning and it said 900 lbs, I would not bat an eye. I feel heavy and slow in my body and mind. As per my morning ritual, I showed up on my mat and worked a few things out. This helped to lessen it, but the thick, sloggy feeling is still lingering.

It's Monday. I can feel an edginess somewhere beneath the surface as I coax my motivation with coffee. I know enough about myself to devise a plan to stay on top of this keen sensitivity. I tell myself, "I'm keeping my eye on you!" I also remind myself that emotions come and go, and as I continue to move through the day, the weightiness will decrease.

If you are alive and reading this, you have likely had a few mornings that you awoke feeling a heaviness. When this happens, please remember that it will pass. Don't let this temporary feeling take over, set the tone for your day, and steal your energy. Take several deep breaths, put your feet on the floor, and start moving. Doing the opposite of what you may want to do will work wonders to bring you back into balance.

Life or Death

Intention: Go easy
Release: Emotional & mental energy

I was standing outside in my socks with no coat. I felt the snow crunching and melting under my feet and fresh flakes wafting down on my face as I looked up at the night sky.

My trip to the outside garbage was refreshing and other-worldly. I was hours into deep emotional and mental interactions with my son. He said he decided tonight was the night he would end his life.

We have had other conversations about this since his accident, but I felt the finality in my heart and heard it in his voice. All of my years and training in suicide prevention came forward as I asked him questions to understand how far along he was with a plan. The why, how, and when were all lined out. Well, shit! I told him several times that at any point, he could change his mind.

There is no joy in making life and death decisions or being with someone whose suffering leads them to this terrible fork in the road. There is no space for judgment or control at this juncture. There is space for love and honesty though. The night passed, and this morning, my son's story continues in this life. I'm relieved and grateful. Today is a good day to go easy and make my holistic rituals a priority. It's time to move the intense energy out through breathing, twisting, squeezing, folding, and screaming if needed.

Many of us have experienced trauma or are close to someone who has. It can be brutal, and the aftermath is felt in every cell of our being. Please go easy. Don't push yourself, blame yourself, or blame the other person. Instead, do every nourishing and nurturing practice to move that energy so it doesn't steal your joy or health. Talk to someone you trust. Journal. Rest. Move. Take a walk. Give yourself the best care.

Changing Plans

Intention: Trust my intuition
Release: Anxiousness

I'm driving down a winding road, mostly in the middle of nowhere. There's a winter storm warning left over from last night. There's a good amount of snow all around, and the skies are dark and gray. In this window of time, it's not actively snowing, but the roads are slippery and snow-packed as I make the short trek to pick up my daughter. I thought the weather would cause us to cancel our plans.

Here, the winter weather can feel like a disrupter when storms come through. I realize how many events and activities I have on my calendar when I have to cancel and reschedule. If the snow continues through the week, and the wind creates blizzard conditions as forecasted, then it's possible that my client will need to cancel her session today. It's also possible that I won't make it back on time or at all on the crappy roads. And then, of course, it will be snowing tomorrow, too, and I may need to make more schedule changes.

Again, winter storms can feel like disruptions. But you know, disruptions aren't necessarily a bad thing. I can get really caught up keeping to a schedule. I am much better at not overloading my time these days, but having my plans derailed leaves me feeling irritated. And when I have to wait to see how things pan out before deciding, it's like being left on hold awaiting the next customer service representative.

My point is that planning takes a lot of energy, and disruptions make me feel anxious. Isn't that just like life as a whole though? We make plans and suddenly, we have to change our direction. What we thought we would do is off the table or left up in the air. It can be very frustrating. It may leave us feeling ungrounded and a little bit disconnected.

Today, my plan is to trust my intuition. If things need to happen, and I feel that subtle sensation in my gut, I will make them happen. And if it doesn't feel quite right, I'll follow that path. I'll try not to get so caught up in my scheduling or allow myself to succumb to anxiousness. Taking it a step further, I'll trust that in the big picture, these changes are a small thing.

It's my hope that you recognize life's disruptions for what they are—just a change of plans. Setting yourself free from the bonds of a plan is great training for being in the moment. Either your schedule works out or it doesn't. Life goes on. You can trust your intuition. You can trust that the sun will rise on another day and once again, you'll move forward on your journey.

Rich & Abundant

Intention: Acknowledge
Release: Forgetfulness

It's another snowy day, and although I was able to meet all of my appointments yesterday, I'm not sure if I'll need to cancel my evening class. Even though I'm waiting out the weather again to make that decision, I can't help but think about how yesterday was rich and abundant beyond what I expected.

Here are a few things I would like to acknowledge from yesterday: safe travels, time with my daughter, an amazing session with a client, holding my brand new grandpuppy, watching my two-year-old granddaughter and the puppy playing, my son having a good day, a stretch of time where the house was full, noisy, and filled with joy, a refrigerator full of healthy foods, a loving, supportive friend and partner to share in all of this abundance.

I'm writing these treasures out in addition to my gratitude list today to remind me that I am supported in the most miraculous and sometimes unexpected ways. Although the road to this point in life has been riddled with potholes, detours, and even closures, I have an incredible life. The good outweighs the bad by leaps and bounds. This exercise has left me feeling humble and deeply thankful. Yeah, I'll just let the tears flow now.

We are quite the experts when it comes to identifying what we don't like about life, which is why we can often think that it's mostly gloom and doom. This is an inherent human quality. To override our focus on the negative, we can switch gears by training our brains to dial in on the positive. A simple and effective way to do this is to write down three to five things that you are grateful for each day. If you crawl into bed and realize you forgot to write them, list them in your mind before you go to sleep. If you're not sold on the merits of a gratitude practice, type "benefits of gratitude research" into a Google search.

Another Lesson

Intention: Grounding
Release: Attachment to plans

Ugh! I did it again. I tried too hard to make my plans work and ended up canceling in the end anyway.

Somehow, I have found myself all worked up over disrupted plans. I guess that means that I need to take a closer look and figure out what happened. There's a piece of this lesson I've missed … *again!* Dammit anyway!

If you are familiar at all with doshas, you'll understand when I say I'm primarily pitta. Pitta energy can be sharp and fiery when imbalanced. I rolled around in this energy for about an hour and then realized I had to bail. I had to reduce or eliminate the pressure I was putting on myself, and not give my family a reason to toss me out in the snowbank.

Today, I'm going to pause periodically to breathe deeply and ground out the remnants of fire still lingering in my body. I'll also be out on the trail among the trees to take in nature's sweet therapy. Should the day go in a different direction, I'm getting ahead of it by mentally and emotionally releasing all of today's plans now and staying open to what the present brings.

How about you? Do you get tied up in your well-planned days and upset when a wrench is thrown in their midst? I feel your pain! Consider simple belly breathing as a way to recenter and ground your energy. Deep, belly breathing is calming because of the way it shifts us into the parasympathetic or the rest and digest part of the nervous system. Being in nature has this effect too. In addition, telling our mind that we can flow with whatever changes come our way before our plans are dashed, prepares us to face such possibilities with more ease.

Loving-Kindness Meditation

Intention: Kindness
Release: Self-criticism

The long, cold winters in Wyoming can be a huge challenge for me. Currently, the temperature is 5°F with a real feel of -14°F and is forecasted to continue downward. For the next three days, I will be held hostage indoors by Mother Nature.

I've always thought that people who live in northern areas like here are tough! Winters are as I described already, and summer can creep up to 100° F or more. That's quite a span of temperatures for a person to adapt. But back to winter. How I'm impacted by the season varies along with its intensity. When I lived by myself, it didn't take long to feel depressed. Living with other people changes the effect in a positive way, but being cooped up for more than one day is still hard for me.

Between menopause and winter, I've put on a few pounds. I don't know many women who aren't self-conscious about weight, and then throw in aging. My inner voice has been making snide comments about the extra baggage and her perspective is so engrained in my being that I can barely push back. Being fit and at an ideal weight is part of my identity, a part I'm not ready to give up. I'm glad about that, but the critical narrative has to go.

Maintaining a healthy weight is important, but a healthy mind is equally important. It's time for all of us, women and men, to take a kind approach to our bodies. We cannot hope for a positive outcome when we bully, criticize, and shame ourselves.

Starting today, try adding extra loving-kindness meditation moments. Repeat these nurturing phrases out loud or to yourself each time your inner judge pipes up. "May I be happy and peaceful. May I be healthy and strong. May I be safe and protected from inner and outer harm. May I be filled with ease."

COLLECTION 10

Thinking

Rest

Intention: Preparation
Release: The week ahead

Ahhhh … sleeping in on a frozen Sunday is good therapy. My mornings last week were a true struggle, and I'm grateful to finally feel rested in my mind, body, and soul.

One might think that I had little say about my sleep schedule, but that's not true. I admit that I long for the days my mom would send me to bed and insist on lights out no later than 9 p.m. At fifty-five years old, I should have the discipline to manage my bedtime, yet it's still a challenge. It's days like today that renew my aspirations to take good care of myself and prepare for the week with the incredibly important activity of resting.

Preparation for anything is best started with fresh mental, physical, emotional, and spiritual energy. Most imbalances can be worked out through resting, and those remaining can be managed through movement and stillness. This is an incredible aspect of yoga. When I first started practicing yoga, I was fascinated by the feeling of having worked out and enjoyed a massage simultaneously. My mind and body were calm and relaxed, yet clear and energized. Over the years, my practice has deepened and softened, and I am so much better for it.

Getting the right sleep is important to prepare for the day and week ahead. Having a daily practice of yoga prepares us for the days, weeks, and years ahead. Both are essential activities with cumulative benefits. The sooner we start, the longer we get to enjoy better health.

What is one thing you can do today to prepare your mind, body, and soul for what's ahead? Five minutes of belly breathing? An appropriate bedtime? Learn a new yoga posture? Meditate for five minutes? Why not make this one thing a daily practice?

Big Picture

Intention: Pace myself
Release: Doing it all!

I have a full day ahead—errands and appointments in different communities. Although still frigid, the sun was shining warmly through the windows. My ride will be here right as I finish with my son's morning routine, and I'll be off and running.

In reality, I'm looking forward to getting out and about. It's kind of rare for me these days. I feel energized and on task. My daughter, her boyfriend, and their new puppy arrived at the appointed time to pick me up. We chatted and sipped coffee enroute until it was time to drop them off. I enjoyed some puppy time while they took care of business. It was the makings of an amazing day!

Interestingly, about half of my day's plan came to fruition. I felt frustrated with the first disappointment … and the second. And then, I finally got a grasp of the big picture. The light came on, and I recalled my intention. Realizing that completing my list was not an option, I headed to my favorite coffee shop and ordered my usual half-caf Americano. I sat contentedly with steam flowing from my cup and opened my laptop to knock out a few creations before my one remaining appointment. I acknowledged myself for successfully embodying today's intention and release.

Are you a "do it all" kind of gal? Try pacing yourself today and take yourself off the hook! Maybe you'll leave a few things undone, but you will give yourself time to soak in some moments of not doing anything. Perfect!

Honor What Is

Intention: Back on track
Release: Sloggy energy

There's something about waking to an alarm when it's dark and cold. Personally, I don't find that "something" very motivating.

I managed to get myself moving and made my way to the mat. Now to work out the sloggy, slow, dense energy that greeted me upon waking. Of course, the opposite is needed to find a centered and grounded balance. Today's practice has full breaths, backbends, forward folds, and side lunges, not to mention forearm planks. This should do the trick and help me get back on track mentally, physically, and emotionally.

I'm back in my routine now and feeling much clearer and more motivated. However, I still sense an underlying heaviness in my body and fog in my mind, which I will respect. Hey, I'm up and going. I'll accept that this is how I am today and honor myself with more breaks as needed.

How are you feeling today? Energized? Great! Moving slow? Take care of yourself by breathing fully and moving intentionally. Be curious and compassionate with yourself. Honor what is by taking breaks more often to move and breathe. It's what you need to regain your whole balance.

Deciding

Intention: Open to opportunities
Release: Knowing

The start of a new month at the beginning of a new year makes me feel more optimistic than usual. Beginnings are exciting, although they can be scary, too.

In my experience, having your own business requires having a keen radar for opportunities. But opportunities rarely fall into your lap. They are created and tracked down through trying something new, having an open mind, and seeing potential and possibilities all around. There's a certain amount of vulnerability involved too, and that's risky business. But the alternative is to be safe and miss out on the really cool stuff.

Taking chances is necessary, but not the willy-nilly kind. Before we step into a new endeavor, it's wise to first consider the best- and worst-case scenarios. The questions to answer are, "Can I live with the worst-case scenario?" and "Is the investment worth the best-case scenario?" Most of us cringe at the possibility of failure. It's not as likely that the outcomes of our decisions land in the extremes of best or worst. It's more probable to land somewhere in between. But if the answer to both of the above questions is "yes," then it's time to roll. Although what lies ahead is still unknown, we can move forward with confidence, having already accepted the result.

Have you been timid about exploring opportunities around you? Are you afraid you'll fail? Are you afraid to succeed? Is it all about results? I like to consider all that I learn in the process, which makes every outcome a win. Today, ask yourself the questions above in relation to an opportunity that piques your interest. If it's a green light, it's time to roll! Stay open and embrace the excitement in not knowing where it will lead.

Take a Chance

Intention: Think BIG
Release: Limitations

Lately, I've been thinking a lot about taking chances. I can't say I regret any that I've taken so far, as each has brought me to this place and made me who I am today.

Over the past couple of years, I've taken many, many risks. I left my job to start my business in the midst of Covid. I let myself be seen more than any other time in my life through teaching and social media. I started a new relationship. That's a lot of vulnerability, especially for me. It was scary! I took these chances because I knew I had to in order to reach my goals.

My journey began well before I left my job or met someone wonderful. I had to become a person who was willing to be vulnerable. Over the space of years and countless experiences, I was led through a progression of internal changes. It was a long haul from being an insecure people-pleaser to feeling confident and secure in my own skin. I needed to learn new skills and discover my innate gifts. I had to walk away from old habits, relationships, and beliefs that limited me before I could think BIG.

What's holding you back from your dreams? Identify one habit, one relationship, and one belief that is limiting you. Now, work toward clearing each roadblock. Take the chance. We have this one life, and it's time to think and live BIG.

Is it a Priority?

Intention: Prioritize
Release: Bullshit

I awoke groggy and sighed when I saw the dark lines under my eyes. For me, less than seven hours of sleep means my energy is limited today.

My practice this morning was challenging, but I needed to blast through the energetic blocks and get things circulating. I usually don't schedule clients in the morning because I'm not always certain about the timing of my son's morning routine. But today I have a client coming, and I'm doing my best to focus on what is most important.

I don't know about you, but I can be distracted and end up down a rabbit trail in a nanosecond. God help me! Instead of using the "Does it bring me joy?" measurement, I'm implementing the "Is it a priority?" measurement. I really can't afford any squirrel moments, so the bullshit has to go. It feels better to knock out the priorities and then take a well-deserved break. As a procrastinator, this is a perfect practice for me.

Are you on a tight schedule today? Do you have deadlines on the horizon? Give the "Is it a priority?" measurement a try to clear the path to tackling what's most important first and release the bullshit. Begin with a cleansing breath. Inhale through your nose and sigh out the exhale through an open mouth. You've got this! We've got this!

Lighten Up

Intention: Lightness
Release: Weighty matters

The past two weeks have felt serious and heavy. It's time to take a break from the weight of life circumstances and welcome the sweeter, silly aspects of living.

Today the sun is shining, and the temperature is supposed to be around 40°F. A little sunshine and thawing mean a lot in February in this part of the country. Weatherwise and emotionally, it has been cloudy and uncomfortable. Mostly, I'm able to accept and embody life as it is. It has been almost eight months since my son's accident, and I'm gradually adding more back into my personal and professional schedule. It's a challenging puzzle and honestly, kind of scary to obligate myself and re-enter normal life.

It's Saturday and a great day to get outside, have coffee with my sweetheart, and be silly. Yes, I have some responsibilities to tackle, but I'm mentally and emotionally tossing the heavy stuff overboard. It's a day to lighten the load, raise the sails, and feel the breeze and sun on my face.

If you are feeling weighed down by life, why not give yourself a time-out from mental and emotional burdens? A great way to do this is to make it your intention and move your body. Do something fun. Do something you love that makes you feel light and free. Maybe you can even try something new.

Sneaky Mind

Intention: Watch my thinking patterns
Release: Stories

It's one of those amazing, slow, lazy Sundays. First, waking later than usual and falling back to sleep multiple times. Finally, I'm sipping coffee in bed while I journal.

My week ahead is full of extras almost every day, all the way through to next Sunday. I could easily let my thoughts roam and be filled with tension. But it's my rest and preparation day. I'm paying attention to my thinking and all those sneaky ways my mind can work to blow things up. These old patterns created well-worn paths in my brain and may have served me in the past, but now they just make me anxious.

For the past eight years, I have been on an intentional journey to change my life, beginning with one of the most powerful influences … my mind. The stories I used to tell myself were defeating and really had no basis in reality. Most of those stories kept me small and afraid and stole the joy and peace of living in the present moment. I've changed my way of thinking and learned to be in the here and now, but there are still times when I feel the pull of those old patterns. Thankfully, I have great tools to hold me in the experience of now or bring me back quickly when I drift.

Do you ever pay attention to your thoughts and the stories you tell yourself? Take time today to watch and notice how often you check out of the present moment. If your mind often spins on anxious, defeating stories, take note. Create an affirmation to interject these thoughts or try this one: I am present and peaceful. Each time your mind drifts, take a full breath and repeat this affirmation.

Embracing Age

Intention: Accentuate the positive
Release: Fear of aging

Transitioning into menopause is not for wimps—nor is winter in Wyoming! In my experience, both can be unpredictable and seem to last far too long.

It feels draining to experience both of these internal and external forces at the same time. Although winter is familiar to me, aging has been so very subtle up until recently. There are times when I embrace, even make light of the graying hair, wrinkles, and hot flashes. Other times, I sense an overwhelming fear trying to well up.

I've always thought I would have a mane of gray curls (which may still be) but for now, it's part gray and part my younger hair color. Strange! My body feels and moves differently. I'm not as slim and toned as I used to be. And then there's the fear of becoming obsolete over time, like old technology.

It's tempting to think only of the challenges, but that's just half of the picture, not to mention it's quite skewed. My mom once told me that one of the great parts of getting old was that you could say about anything and get away with it. I'm not that old … yet! On a more serious note, she insisted that each decade was better than the last.

I believe there are plenty of positives to aging, like not giving a crap about what other people think and being at ease in your own skin. There's a gradual slowing down to take life in fully. We are more likely to see and take advantage of opportunities and less likely to procrastinate. We are more considerate of our health and have more compassion for ourselves and others as we know the storms we have come through. Our boundaries are firm for the same reason. With decades of knowledge and experience under our belts, we have a greater capacity to love.

Here's where I will leave you for the day—with just a few of the amazing gifts of aging. Let's embrace the gray (if that's your thing!), the curves, and the fear of growing old. For all we know, the best is yet to come.

Habit of Showing Up

Intention: Posture
Release: What doesn't work

How we show up for life is important. But the fact that we show up regardless of how we feel is an act of bravery.

We call yoga a practice because it's where we challenge ourselves in various ways and get to know who we are in the process. Yoga is a tool to connect with every part of ourselves. The first step is to show up on the mat and bring awareness to the breath. We take one posture and feel powerful. We take another and feel vulnerable. With our breath connecting movement to stillness and engagement to pause, we sense, feel, and observe. With each breath and posture, we gradually release what doesn't work.

The embodied experience on the mat prepares us for the yoga of life—the twists, folds, holds, transitions, and releases. We face and move through what we like and don't like and manage what requires all of our strength and focus. Each practice welcomes us where we are in the moment. We have the opportunity to learn deeper awareness and acceptance and to become curious as we breathe it all in, knowing that we can accept pleasant and unpleasant alike as each will pass.

Whether we want to show up to practice or life, by doing so, we create the habit. We move through the postures, letting go of what doesn't work. We continue to show up! In time, we become people who show up for ourselves and for others. Because not showing up simply doesn't work.

COLLECTION 11

Healing

Semi-Colon Day

Intention: Pause
Release: Hurries & worries

On and around full moons, I either find myself buzzing with energy or depleted. Unfortunately, this time, I'm mentally and physically worn out.

I tend to make more mistakes when I feel tired because my mind is foggy and my body clumsy. There is a need to slow everything down and really pay attention. I prefer this approach to fixing mistakes that I inevitably make when I ignore the state of my being. My day will be sprinkled with semi-colons. I'll pause often to take an extra look and a full breath before proceeding. It may be that I leave certain tasks for another day, but that's perfectly fine. No hurries, no worries.

How would it feel to gift yourself grace when you feel tired in your mind and body? Do you tend to show yourself kindness and speak to yourself with compassion, or do criticism and impatience rule on these days? I encourage you to slow down and treat yourself with sweetness like you do a true friend. Pause. Breathe. Proceed with love.

Energy Inventory

Intention: Use energy wisely
Release: Background tension

Between the aftermath of the full moon and my rogue perimenopausal hormones, my gas tank is running low. But, as nature would have it, it's not that simple.

I recently learned that when progesterone levels are low, which is common in PM (perimenopausal) women, one is more likely to experience anxiety. Of course, anxiety is associated with the sympathetic nervous system (fight, flight, or freeze) and the body produces more stress hormones, like cortisol and adrenaline. This general feeling of anxiousness makes it easy to be further triggered by daily challenges. Good lord, no wonder I'm a hot mess!

Do you have apps on your cell phone? Me too! (Probably too many.) Periodically, my phone dings with a notification that an app hasn't been used in a while, and it would like to put it into a deep sleep. This is because the app is using resources that shorten the battery charge. This is not unlike the nervous system.

I think my underlying anxiety is comparable to an app running in the background, slowly eking away my limited resources. But as much as I would like to be put into a deep sleep, it's a workday, and apparently, I'm an adult with responsibilities. With that in mind, my approach today is to use my energy wisely. Lower energy days are just part of this season and life transition.

Are you aware of what affects your energy? On days when your reserves are low, do you push yourself until your battery is all but dead? Take time today to inventory where you spend your energy. Are there tasks or people that you can postpone until the higher energy days? If you're experiencing perimenopause or menopause, be sure to have your hormone levels checked so you have a good understanding of why you may be feeling less energized.

Note: Feeling calm and present is a characteristic of the parasympathetic nervous system. Spending quiet time alone is an essential tool to tap into this restful state and reduce anxiousness.

Gather the Sprinkles

Intention: Feel the joy
Release: Heavy emotions

Even in the greatest difficulties, there are sprinkles of joy. It may take everything we have not to let ourselves be blinded to it, but that's exactly what we must do.

Have you gone through (or are you in) a time of life where tough circumstances seem to drag on and on? At some point, we must make the decision on how we perceive hard experiences. Will we be sucked into a dark emotional hole, or will we gather the sprinkles of joy? In reality, we make this choice many times over the days, months, and years. It's not that we can't visit dark places; it's just not in our best interest to stay too long.

So squint, strain, or ask someone with better vision to help, but find and gather the sprinkles. It may not be the joy that blows you over on your ass and leaves you breathless, but nevertheless, you may feel a flash of warmth and lightness in your heart. These little sprinkles are reminders that you will come through this challenge just as you have all the others.

Feel Into Life

Intention: Feel into what I do
Release: Trying to make sense of things

I've long been curious about the much-used yoga teacher verbiage of "felt sense" and "feel into." Feel into your breath, your body, or the pose. Notice the felt sense. Actually, all of life can be experienced as a felt sense, meaning that it can be an embodiment, not just thought or emotion.

I spend a good deal of time and energy trying to sort out why things happen and nailing down a reason for the timing. In some instances, I'm satisfied to just let it feel like magic. But, more often than not, I want answers! This approach sets me up for some disappointments and frustrations as it's more likely that I will be left wondering rather than piecing together a complete picture.

It's my intention today to be more aware of my thoughts and actions, especially noticing how my body feels in the moment. I will pay attention to how my body responds to various tasks, news, and conversations. Am I breathing fully? Am I squeezing my shoulders up to my ears? Did I just feel a flash of nausea? Is my face relaxed? Am I slouching? Am I rigid? These inquiries get me out of my head and into my body. Connected. Grounded. Present.

We get a lifetime to learn about ourselves, but there are no guarantees of how long that really is. Spending our precious time spinning on a mental gerbil wheel keeps us busy, anxious, and out of touch as we try to make sense of things. Let's show ourselves some love today by having more than just a mental-emotional workout. Let's have the whole experience, one that is felt by all our senses. One that we feel in our bodies.

Choices

Intention: Duality – Holding space for two things
Release: Worry

Being stuck between two choices, two directions, or two possibilities can be stressful. Although the tension may eventually reach a crescendo, just as in most classical music pieces, the intensity gradually subsides and is followed by a lightness. The decision has been made.

I worry more about a decision where I have to wait to see where the final options fall. During the waiting period, I tend to make up stories about how things will play out. It can be helpful to be prepared for the two likely outcomes of a situation. This is where I grind my teeth. In my mind, I grumble about the extra work and about the mental-emotional space not knowing takes up.

I'm facing one of those situations today … again. Being mindful that there are two possibilities, I will use my energy to prepare for both and do my best to hold space for these scenarios. Why worry when I'm ready for either? The truth is that I would be worrying if I wasn't making a mindful effort to accept either outcome. Just as I did yesterday, I'm paying attention to how my thoughts and emotions feel in my body.

Are you worrying about the outcome of a situation? Consider the two most likely scenarios. Then, breathe in fully to create space for both, and breathe out completely to release the energy of worry. It's going to work out exactly how it needs to work out.

Unlearning

Intention: Healing practices - tension
Release: Physical-emotional blocks

Have you noticed that when you feel tension, it's often in the same physical areas? If there is stress, no matter its origin, our muscles and joints are trained to respond.

The tightness in my neck and shoulder muscles is remarkable today. Part of it is stress, and part is my need to visit my chiropractor. I've been catching myself with my shoulders lifted toward my ears. Each time, I take a deep breath as I squeeze them even tighter, then slowly lower and roll them back and down with a mindful exhale. This is how I am retraining my brain and muscles to communicate. It's a neuromuscular practice that addresses the somatic nervous system. Somatic movements play an important role in reprogramming how spinal and cranial nerves speak to various muscles, and this supports healing.

Having lived much of my life in the fight or flight stress response, I am slowly unlearning and unwinding. I acknowledge myself for prioritizing my health and well-being more and more over the years. This progress is revealed each time I face a challenge. Instead of dumping into my sympathetic nervous system and anxiously hanging out, I typically make a quick visit. Then, I apply those amazing healing practices that have taught me how to accept what is and move on. Somatic movement is one of many tools for which I am forever grateful.

What are your go-to practices? Are they healing you? Could you use a new tool? Either seated or standing, take a deep breath in through your nose as you squeeze your shoulders up toward your ears. Hold the tension and your breath for a couple of seconds. As you breathe out through your mouth, roll your shoulders back and down. Pause any movement as you take two more full breaths, further releasing your shoulders. Now gently shake your arms, hands, and fingers (legs and feet as well) to cast off any lingering blocks.

Mental Rx

Intention: Healing practices - thoughts
Release: Criticism

As humans, we have incredible minds! We can revisit the past and dream about the future in a flash of seconds. Our imaginations generate ideas, create stories, and fill in the blanks.

One possible issue with all of this creativity is that our perceptions and memories are tainted by how we view the world. In other words, we interpret and remember things as we are, not necessarily as they happened in reality. If we think we're not good enough, our self-talk supports that theme and the stories we tell ourselves paint us (and oftentimes others) in a poor light. Our recollections can be painful, and our critical self-perception keeps us from dreaming. We end up stuck as our anxious thoughts deepen the dark neuropathways while they cycle through on repeat.

Just as we can retrain and heal our muscles, we can do the same with our thoughts. To unlearn old thought habits and get out of spinning patterns, we can introduce a positive replacement. If your default thinking (that which comes without any effort) is detrimental, it's high time to start a mantra or affirmation practice. In time and with practice, these positive statements will not only replace the old, but you will embody their essence. If your affirmation is, "I am healthy and strong," you will be more likely to make choices that contribute to those outcomes.

The first step is to become aware of your self-talk as well as the stories you tell yourself. This requires you to be still, be quiet, and listen. Meditation is a perfect tool for this part. Once you figure out your go-to self-judgments and the erroneous stories you've been telling yourself, it's time to either create or find an affirmation that counters the negative. It should be short and in the present.

As an example, the affirmation above would be perfect if you find yourself playing the victim in your stories or your inner voice criticizes you for always being sick and weak. Your Rx is: I am healthy and strong. Repeat repeatedly!

Free Therapy

Intention: Healing practices - nature
Release: The world

"Nature itself is the best physician."

—Hippocrates

Growing up in the Black Hills, I've always loved being in nature. Even as a young girl, I would go out exploring with my dog Smoky. We would roam around the acres surrounding our home for the entire day or until we were thirsty and/or hungry. Coming from a large family, I appreciated the peacefulness and privacy of being alone in the woods. When I returned home after my nature adventures, I felt content, calm, energized, and like I had just experienced something wonderful that words could not describe, and others may not understand.

As an adult, I've come back to my roots in the Hills. Just as when I was a child, I continue to be drawn into the trees, uphill to the highest points, making my way on familiar paths and soaking in the beauty of each season. Sometimes, I travel on foot, sometimes on snowshoes, and other times, on a mountain bike.

Until two years ago, I made these sojourns with my best friend and four-legged adventurer, Spocky. Her final resting place is in a grove of oak trees on our property. Regardless of what's going on in my life or in the world, I have always returned from nature better than when I entered her healing realm.

What is your relationship with nature? When was the last time you wandered on her therapeutic paths? With so much unrest in the world, take up nature on her offer to heal you.

Catalyst for Healing

Intention: Healing practices - expression
Release: Inhibitions

We are all wired with creative energy, so if you're someone who says, "I don't have a creative bone in my body," please hear me out.

Our inventive minds (and opposable thumbs) set us apart from other beings. We all come with our own unique ways of expressing ourselves. Some people dance, others sew, and others paint or bake. The way we walk and dress provides small glimpses into our individuality. For all of the estimated 117 billion people that have lived on this earth, there are multiple times more ways of creative expression.

I cannot tell you how many times I have come to a point in the publishing process of this book where I told myself that I have nothing unique to offer. The fact is, I do. And you do, too. You have wonderful ways of expressing that are all your own. And when you and I allow them to flow out, the world is blessed by our contributions. And if that's not enough, this expression is not just entertainment, but a catalyst for healing.

Grab your journal! Today, explore ways that you express yourself. Make a list and write about how each expression makes you feel. Be bold and uninhibited! What you discover is a key to healing.

Stop, Calm, Rest, Heal

Intention: Healing practices - rest
Release: Pushing too hard

Rest is one of the most underrated modes of healing. How can so much be accomplished by doing nothing?

Thích Nhất Hạnh, a well-known Buddhist monk and spiritual leader taught that healing requires these three practices: stopping, calming, and resting.[2] I have been learning how impactful it is to hit the pause button, especially when I don't want to. Of course, that's when I need it most! But it's important that the pause is a thoughtful engagement of the mind, body, and soul. The need to stop is preceded by an encounter with mental, emotional, or physical angst or pain.

When I stop pushing too hard, I can detect the distress I'm experiencing. This provides the opportunity to take a closer look. Usually, I discover it's not such a scary monster when I bring it from the mental closet into the light. This leads to the next step—calming. I see the issue as it is rather than how I perceived it through my anxiousness. Now, I am able to accept it. Acceptance does not mean that I have to like or dislike it; it simply means I understand the issue and that it exists.

I've now reached the state where I can truly rest. My nervous system shifts down, and my breathing slows. I experience awareness and acceptance together. My thoughts leave the past and future to settle into the present moment. I have reached the healing space.

Do you tend to push too hard? Put the wisdom of Thích Nhất Hạnh into practice today by stopping, calming, and resting. As a reminder, write these healing steps on a sticky note and place it where you'll see it often. Or take a picture of that note and make it the background on your computer or cell phone.

COLLECTION 12

Simplifying

Slow Down

Intention: Easy does it
Release: Hangover

I've noticed that as I move deeper into my 50s, that a highly active day followed by not quite enough sleep feels a little like a hangover. My knowledge of hangovers comes from a reliable source—my younger self!

I was on a GSD spree of epic proportions yesterday. If you're not familiar with this acronym, it stands for Get Shit Done. It has long been my life motto and modus operandi. Even though I have tamed this deeply ingrained tendency by pausing more to stop, breathe, and rest, I have my days and moments of rogue GSD energy. Yesterday, for example. Although I'm grateful for a clean, organized home, I'm worn out.

Today, I will nurse my GSD hangover by moving more slowly and resting more often. I'll stop to enjoy a cup of tea, breathe, and be present for the experiences today brings. I'll use this physical reminder to inform my decisions going forward and mindfully pace myself. In this season of life, I am blessed with the option and prodded by the wisdom of my body to take it easy. I'm listening.

My dear sister, could you use a down day to nurse a hangover? You got it! If your inner critic has something to say, tell her that she gets the day off too.

Plan B

Intention: Make the best of what is
Release: Not getting what I wanted

"Being hopeful doesn't always get us what we want," says Captain Obvious. There are variables that influence the direction and outcomes of our days and our lives. Some we can control, and others are in the hands of the unknown.

My partner and I haven't gone out of town together since my son's accident, which was eight months ago. So, we made plans to fly a few hours away and stay the night, attend an award presentation for my sweetie, and come home the next day. My daughter had arranged to stay with my son. It was a short, sweet dream dashed by a winter storm. Plan B is to stay home and make the best of things.

I really wanted the break of going to sleep and waking up without anyone to take care of besides myself. This beautiful, but tiring experience of shifting closer to menopause has worn me thin, made me very sensitive, and caused me to feel "old" for the first time in my life.

I went to sleep at the age of fifty, where the world was my oyster, and woke up at fifty-five, seeing my mom in the mirror. I'm in another dimension where Harrison Ford is eighty, Bruce Willis has dementia, and my hair is gray. No one really ever told me about this part of life. And who knows, maybe I wouldn't have wanted to hear about it.

But I'm willing to make the best of what is. Staying home. Getting on board with this wise transition that will eventually lead me into the season of menopause. For now, it feels like a storm. Thankfully, storms always pass. Being disappointed because of canceled plans doesn't necessarily have to be a disappointment. It can simply be a brief moment in time that leaves behind a very rare thing—empty space.

Think about a time when you were upset because plans fell through and you didn't get what you wanted. What was your reaction? Were you able to make the best of things? If so, acknowledge yourself. If not, how would you respond today?

Listen to Your Body

Intention: Down time
Release: Weariness

For real this time! I'm calling myself out for not resisting the urge to push when my body and energy said rest.

Since I can remember, checking the weather forecast has been an important step in scheduling, especially during the season when there are only windows of "good" weather. I love being outdoors in all seasons, but it takes planning to get out when the weather is ideal.

During the winter, I love snowshoeing on a snowy day, like yesterday. The temperature was reasonable, the snow was deep and falling steadily. It was beautiful! The tree branches were adorned with four to six inches of fresh snow and small icicles clung to them as the wind gusted. Deep in the oak grove and protected from the wind, my partner and I plopped into the comfy snow for a break. Lying back, we watched the snow swirl as we soaked in the magical forest.

It's not that these adventures aren't fulfilling, it's that I pushed too hard. Instead of feeling rested and recovered this morning, I am weary. This business of learning to turn the dial down is really challenging for me, but I feel in my body that I have no other choice if I want to be well. Listening to my body and planning accordingly just makes good sense. Change can sometimes be hard, right?!

Are you an overdoer? Or are you an underdoer? Either way, listening to your body and your inner wisdom is the key to wellness. This requires a thoughtful approach of compassion and kind persuasion. If your tendency is to move to exhaustion, then rest. If your tendency is idleness, then add movement. If you keep at it, you will tap into your personal rhythm.

Mostly Okay

Intention: Watch & listen
Release: Resistance

"It's actually quite a good ethos for life: go into the unknown with truth, commitment, and openness, and mostly you'll be okay."

–Alan Cumming

What I really like about this quote is its integrity. This space of time I occupy was once unknown to me, and I have been mostly okay. Truthfully, there is much about it I still don't understand. So, even though I'm standing here in time, much of the landscape is still quite foreign and unfamiliar.

Aging, perimenopause, caregiver, partner, grandmother, solopreneur, home builder, teacher, healer, writer … These are just a few pieces of my current landscape. Again, some are familiar, and some are surreal.

I recall my Anatomy & Physiology college professor saying that hormones make up the personality. As I listen to the audiobook version of *Wise Power*[3] with that statement in mind, I'm somewhat fearful. Although I'm still on the outskirts of menopause, I'm concerned about who I will be when the dust settles.

For now, I will watch and listen as an observer of myself. As we all must, I'm moving forward. It's like being on an escalator where even if you stop, you're still moving. How curious to see myself from a couple of steps back. I notice where I resist to no avail. The best course is to approach today and each day with "truth, commitment, and openness" to conserve my energy for the moments and years ahead—for the unknown.

P.S. I highly recommend reading or listening to *Wise Power*[4] by Alexandra Pope and Sjanie Hugo Wurlitzer, the founders of Red School, especially if your age is forty+. It has so much useful information to support you through menopause as a spiritual path. Their first book, *Wild Power*, which I have not read yet, offers guidance for embracing menstruation as part of a woman's spiritual path.

Herding the Monkey

Intention: Take the next step
Release: Busy thoughts

Every large endeavor is achieved by focusing on and completing one task at a time.

Sometimes, my biggest barrier to getting things done is having too many projects going on at once and feeling overwhelmed. Indecision taps out my nervous system, and I spin in circles. In my morning meditation and four-part check-in (mind, body, emotions, and spirit), I'd already discovered that my mind was a bit busy.

This is useful information. I gave myself a very grounding, gentle practice on the mat as a result. There's work to be done today, and I want to proceed from the best space possible.

My first task is to list what needs to be done today and prioritize each in order. I'm doing my best to focus on and tackle one to-do at a time, but my mind is easily distracted. Just like with meditation, I gently draw it back to the present moment. It looks like that's just how my day will go—herding my monkey mind back to the present. And it's okay. I'm going to do what I can to pick up where I leave off and breathe well.

We all have days or periods of time when our minds are scattered and busy. It can be caused by a myriad of things like hormones, sleep cycles, lack of or too much exercise, diet, and of course, the stresses of life. Giving ourselves grace goes a long way and may be just what we need to support ourselves to take the next step. Just one step, then the next. We can draw our attention back to what's at hand, and then move forward again. By speaking kindly and breathing fully, we will get the job done.

Knowing Better

Intention: A day for me
Release: Guilt

It's been a very long time since I had a day to myself and although that isn't in the cards today, I can still carve out time for me.

A day for me includes saying no, going in my room with the door closed to rest, read, or write, choosing something to do just for fun, not cooking, starting on a project I never seem to get to, letting my creative juices flow where they will, walking or snowshoeing, slowing down, playing guitar, singing, laughing more, and generally holding space for myself to just be.

I shake my head as I think about how I let my candle burn so low before taking a day to restore my energy. I know better. I teach others to do this, but somehow, I let self-care slip this week. But I'm back on track. So far, I've slept in and had a full yoga practice to myself. It's a great start!

Next up: A walk in the sunshine to welcome the warmer weather and soak in nature. These are not indulgences. They are absolute necessities, the essentials of health. There is no space for feeling guilty or prioritizing everyone but me. I am recommitting to making myself a priority by weaving self-care into every day this week. My well-being is far too important.

When was the last time you had a day for YOU? And when is the last time you put yourself at the top of the list without feeling guilty? When you do take time for your own needs, remember that you are the number one priority. When your cup is full and you are well, those around you will be blessed by your example and how you contribute to their lives by practicing self-care.

Priority #1: YOU!!

Vote for YOU

Intention: Keep prioritizing myself
Release: Habit of procrastinating self-care

"Every action you take is a vote for the person you wish to become."

—James Clear, Atomic Habits[5]

I listened to *Atomic Habits*, by James Clear, on Audible, then ordered the book. It's one of those books you want to have around to reference, highlight, and fill with sticky notes. It's chock-full of quotable treasures. Because I'm first a yoga practitioner (student) and second a yoga teacher (in that order), I've been training in personal awareness for years. Even so, that does not negate the fact that I veer off course from time to time. This happens when I stop paying attention.

Unfortunately, I've voted many times over the past several months for the person I don't want to become, yet I have invested in her, nonetheless. I've let myself become someone who doesn't get enough rest or take enough quality time alone. I cast a few votes for the self-sacrificing mom and some to the strong and courageous yet vulnerable warrior goddess.

Having thoroughly enjoyed my day yesterday, which I deemed "a day for me," I'm more motivated to support my empowered, kind, badass self who cares for herself first, then others. Monday will come, and I'll have a jumpstart on renewing my habit of self-care.

Have you lost yourself in the busyness of life? Is your physical, mental, and emotional health taking a hit? If so, it's likely that you are not making yourself a priority. Waiting until tomorrow or for that pie-in-the-sky time when all the planets are aligned to start is an illusion. You will never get around to it without just doing something now.

Set your intention to do one thing today and do it. Tomorrow, set the same intention and take the same action. That's right! The day after tomorrow, again, keep the same intention and take the same action. Take the approach that your life depends on this one self-care practice. In reality, it does! String enough todays together, and you will have hundreds, even thousands of votes for the person you truly want to become.

P.S. You are a badass warrior goddess!

Preservatives

Intention: Keep life simple
Release: Fillers & imposters

Simplicity is one of life's most effective stress reducers.

I've been reading food labels for many years and have stopped buying products with ingredients I cannot pronounce, let alone know their definition and purpose. Often, these inclusions are to preserve or simply act as fillers. Fillers just take up space without improving nutritional value. Busyness can also be seen as a filler. It fills spaces of time so one doesn't pause and deal with life. It's a sneaky strategy to make me unavailable in relationships, including with my own sweet self.

Imposters serve the same purpose. When we buy things we don't use or really need, those items become imposters. We create the illusion that we have everything a girl could ever want. The "stuff" stacks up along with the debt, leaving us feeling empty and deceived by the overflowing closet and cluttered house.

The beauty of keeping life simple is that it's … simple. There's a sense of ease and peace. We have the resources and time to live life more leisurely—you know, to stop and smell the roses.

Take time this week to review your life for fillers and imposters. Beat the bushes and shake out the sheets. Find them and give them the boot. It's time to simplify your life.

Holding on Too Long

Intention: Give permission
Release: What my heart has left

If I had a top ten list titled "Things I Learned the Hard Way," it would include how holding on to something or someone when my heart has already moved on makes life miserable.

The fear of free falling into an unknown future has kept me frozen in careers and relationships far beyond their expiration dates. There was often a voice inside that told me if I would just hold on another day, month, or year, the situation might change. At first, this was easy to believe, and I would continue to invest in the status quo. I would give myself a pep talk, jump up and down to get the energy flowing, and dive back in. Each time, my attention span was shorter, my creativity waned, and I needed another pep talk.

I had several roles over the years in family businesses. As much as I wanted a position with fewer hours and less responsibility as a single, widowed mother of four, I stayed at it for fifteen years. During this time, I was in a relationship that was not a good fit. We were on and off more times than I care to remember. I stayed on. I stayed in.

Some days were half-hearted at best. I knew I had to let go of both as my heart certainly had done so. Well, the businesses were sold, and I finally left the relationship, vowing never to overstay in either type of situation again. Those were tough times. Letting go was followed by a free fall into the unknown. It was scary!

After that, I took a job that I would unenthusiastically drive to each morning. As I approached the turn, I would keep going, traveling another few blocks before circling back around to the parking lot. As I did this, I would tell myself that it was valuable experience, less stressful, and I should be grateful to have it since I had four kids at home. Damn, though! I was miserable!

Finally, I gave myself permission to give my notice and begin the next free fall. Weeks later, I was offered a position at a non-profit. This ended up being my career for over twelve years. I loved it … until it reached the expiration date. Once again, I gave myself permission to move on, handing the baton to my replacement. It was time to step into the unknown.

I've had my own business for just over four years now. It hasn't been easy. I've transformed, and as I have, so has my business. But the intention to help others heal is still at the heart of what I do. I feel another letting go on the horizon, although I'm not sure what it is for certain. It's scary, but I'm giving myself permission to move on when my heart is ready.

Take time today to make a mental inventory of your relationships, your work, and other ways you spend your time. As you ponder, write down those things that you feel in your heart have run their course. When your list is complete, write yourself a note giving permission to move on. It may be scary to take action and step into the unknown, but you've got this!

Innate Wisdom

Intention: Be present in the transition & open to self-discovery
Release: Resistance

Making discoveries about oneself requires curiosity and awareness. Accepting these discoveries and having a willingness to change requires courage.

When my kids were young, they would come to me with stories about how something played out. As I listened, I would determine if they were embellishing the details or not. If it seemed a bit far-fetched, I would encourage them to start over, beginning with "once upon a time." Hey, if you're telling a story that is not real, it only seems right to give the listener a clue.

Over my lifetime, I have told myself and others stories. Some were filled with excuses and others were wishes that I had no real intention of following through. But with each year past fifty, I have less and less of a stomach for bullshit—especially my own. Somehow, this shift has made it difficult for me to be open to new possibilities. I see that I am partially closed off, and I'm not quite sure how that happened.

During the first couple of years of my business, I was aligned with my intuitive rhythms. I created strategies and programs and taught with passion and vulnerability. I honestly don't know where it came from, but it just flowed out of me. I felt so free. It seems that the way to the next iteration of me is a rebirth of sorts.

The discovery of feeling closed off has made me curious. Is it time to go within for a period of rest to prepare for a growth spurt? Could it be that I am perfectly in rhythm with my intuition and inner knowing?

There is an innate wisdom at work. I am watching and listening. I am curious. And I am certain that when it's time to be born into the next season, my heart will know. For now, I will accept and make the most of this space between what is finished and what is yet to come.

Do you allow yourself to hover in the discomfort of transitions, or are you inclined to resist? The following meditation will strengthen your capacity to not only sit with difficulties but also examine them to discover more about yourself.

Sit comfortably, close your eyes, and begin belly breathing. When you feel grounded, bring to mind an issue or behavior that has been disturbing your inner peace. Do your best to approach it as an observer, seemingly unattached. Then, ask the issue or behavior what it has come to teach you. Continue to watch, listen, and be curious. After five to ten minutes, place both palms over your heart, and whisper, "I see and honor you, my sweetheart." Then open your eyes. Repeat as often as desired and/or needed.

COLLECTION 13

Shifting

Issues in the Tissues

Intention: Contribute to life & health
Release: Habits of dis-ease

Every choice we make either contributes to health and life or to disease and death. Learning the art of self-awareness puts us in the driver's seat to make the best decisions for our own well-being.

Nothing ever gets past the nervous system. It's the ultimate alarm system—sensitive and highly evolved. Even so, as humans, we have commandeered our conscious mind to override its subtle warnings. To our own demise, we ignore messages meant to protect us and prevent problems.

Until we learn to tune in and take appropriate action, we are following the path of disease. Every time we fail to acknowledge the large and small irritations and devastations of life, we stuff one more "I can't deal with it now" issue in our internal closet until inevitably, it's filled to capacity. All the while, our nervous system is moving up through warning levels until we're in a chronic state of stress, causing other body systems to suffer or fail. As the saying goes, "The issues are in the tissues." That's how it happens.

The moral of this essay is that handling shit as it comes is our ticket to better health. There's no separating physical, mental, emotional, and spiritual health. If one is out of whack, all are impacted.

If your closet is full, there's plenty of hope and help to begin sorting through the trauma, regrets, illness, guilt, shame, and every other issue. Find someone or multiple someones to guide you on your healing journey—teachers, mentors, healers, support groups, counselors, etc. Read or listen to books with topics that resonate with your pain and inspire the desire to free yourself. They're out there because someone else has had a similar experience. There are wonderful groups on social media, too, but be cautious.

My point is that you are not alone, and it's never too late. Now is always the best time to begin sorting out your past and present, change habits that support dis-ease, and create the vibrant, balanced, healthy life you deserve. What is one small action you can take right now to contribute to life and health?

Good Medicine

Intention: Joyful ease
Release: Routine

For the first time in almost nine months, my sweetie and I spent a night away from home! My amazing daughter is hanging out *and caring for* my son, her younger brother, while we spend a night away. After teaching class last evening, we headed thirty miles away to relax.

The terms squeeze and soak are paired in yoga. The squeeze refers to a constriction or hold while the soak is what occurs in the release. In the release, circulation returns, and energy flows freely and even more robustly.

The constriction of the past nine months and the daily squeeze of our altered experience have taken a great deal of our energy. This is not to say that we don't take advantage of any available moment to soak. But time away has certainly been good therapy and a way to move blocked energy. For this brief hiatus, we're out of our routine and enjoying some free flow. It's good medicine and gives me hope for teasing out more joy and ease within each day.

Is it time for you to get out of your regular routine? When was the last time you allowed yourself to soak in the joyful ease available for the taking? Grab the moments, an hour, or a day to step out of the squeeze. It's excellent for physical, mental, emotional, and spiritual circulation.

Protective Shield

Intention: Lean into hope & joy
Release: Others' energy

We are all responsible for our own emotions and behaviors, and that's more than enough.

I'm back at home and enjoying a rather laid-back Saturday so far. I'm excited about the new home we're building and about new possibilities with my business. What's not thrilling me is being around negative energy. I want to feel these summer-like emotions and ride on their warm, fragrant breeze. It's my choice as to what I let in and how I allow myself to be affected by other people's behaviors and emotional energy.

I see boundaries as a protective bubble. I have physical, mental, emotional, and spiritual layers that vary in prominence based on my own state of being, and who or what I'm encountering. It's complicated. For those closest to me, and with whom I feel safe, I allow myself to be more vulnerable. The opposite is true for people I don't have an intimate relationship with. This is where things seem tricky to me. The vulnerability in my closest relationships can expose me to some difficult behaviors and attitudes. In fairness, they are also exposed to the same from me. It's hard to imagine that I'm not always a joy to be around. (This is where you laugh.)

Today, let's hold space for other people's less than desirable moods to run their course. We can lean into and fully feel our own inner hope and joy regardless. Our protective shields are raised with love for self and love for those wrestling with themselves.

Eggshells

Intention: Openness & communication
Release: Being too careful

Quiet is wonderful, but without its companion peace, it becomes unbearable.

Walking on eggshells really sucks! I have traded my openness for silence to avoid the inevitable confrontation. At least that's the way I see it. I really thought I had outgrown this terrible strategy, but here I am.

If you have lived with someone who is angry and often depressed, you can likely relate. There is a part of me that wants to fortify my boundaries, give a hard nudge back, and lay everything out on the table. There's another part that understands approaching the issue with small changes can feel more compassionate. It's similar to the difference between the explosion of popping a balloon or pricking a small hole to allow the air to release slowly.

I'm more prone to having open communication, even with the risk of disagreement, confrontation, and the like. Besides, being too careful has probably never opened the door to real communication in a tense relationship. It's possible that the outcome will be relief and resolution for both of us. Today, I'll take time to prepare my heart and my words, and then start the conversation. Regardless of how it's received, I will proceed with love.

Do you have a challenging relationship that causes you to walk on eggshells? It sucks, right?! Take time today to consider the individual and your relationship with them through the lens of your heart. When you are ready, start the conversation.

Vantage Point

Intention: Take the high ground
Release: Temptation to force

A bigger hammer isn't the solution for most of the problems in life. Although letting someone have it may sound justified and satisfying in our minds, it usually makes things worse.

Being assertive is a way to make our boundaries known. Statements that define what I will do and what I won't do are examples. However, being aggressive or forceful tends to stomp on other people's boundaries. I've learned to stay in my own lane in this area of communication. I'm reminded of a question my yoga teacher asked in training, which was, "Do you want to be right, or do you want the relationship?"

Thinking that we're right in a conflict is a slippery slope to stand on. It's easy to completely lose sight of the person in front of us as we focus on making our point. There's no listening, just the sound of our mind spinning up what to blast them with next. This way of communicating is fueled by emotions and leaves us with regrets and a damaged or lost relationship.

Taking the high ground is an act of standing up for your values, especially when in a tense disagreement. It's more about the approach. Rather than scrapping it out in the ring, take a step back and rise above heated emotions to gain a clearer vantage point. The high ground allows us to see and hear the other person. It positions us to think more clearly, speak mindfully, and be fully present. It's much more likely to incite a discussion rather than an argument.

What circumstances and/or relationships can you improve by taking the higher ground?

See Yourself

Intention: Re-evaluate
Release: Not seeing

I enjoy stepping back to get a better view of myself and my life. I recognize that it's time to re-evaluate and make changes.

We've been through some shit over the past several months, and I'm feeling it in my body. I'm dialing in on the symptoms and evaluating my options. I'm asking myself questions like, "What do you need?" and "How can I support you better?"

On my walk today, I looked back through my life and timeline of traumas that ran on a continuum from mild to major. Some I had all but forgotten, while others were still fresh. It's a lot to take in. By stepping back to be an observer of myself, I cannot help but feel a deep compassion and appreciation. I acknowledge that I've had hard experiences in life and yet, I'm still full of love.

When was the last time you really saw yourself? Ever? For the next few days, set aside time to be an observer of your beautiful, resilient self. See the real you with the utmost compassion and appreciation.

Shifting

Intention: Welcome new season
Release: Winter

Living where there are four distinct seasons is wonderful! The transition from winter to spring is especially exciting!

Today is the spring equinox, and although the ground is still mostly covered in ice and snow, there are small patches where the earth is visible. On my walk the past couple of days, I took time to lay in the soft pine needles and look up at the green branches and blue sky. I dug into the cold soil for a handful and inhaled deeply. It has been a long winter, which is how many of us who live here feel every year.

The seasons are in transition, as am I. Moving from winter to spring is expected and something I've experienced for fifty-five years. But my personal transition is new. I'm uncertain and don't have a bearing on where I'll land. Knowing I'm shifting is actually enough for now. I understand that being actively engaged in the process is important, and when I arrive at the next season, it will feel new, yet natural.

If you are feeling as if life or an area of life is shifting under your feet, take a closer look. Are you simply experiencing a shift? How can you engage in the process and welcome the new season?

Small Differences

Intention: Better habits
Release: Mindless habits

As part of my re-evaluation, I recognize that my body needs more TLC.

Although I practice yoga, walk in nature, and stay hydrated, I've been feeling run down. The sheer amount of stress that comes with being a caregiver, plus menopause and trying to keep my income at least trickling, is a constant hum. My need to discover a balance that lands me on the upside of health has become quite obvious. The dark lines under my eyes and my daily struggle for energy are two standouts.

Over the weekend, I decided to make my sleep a priority. I cut off coffee earlier, eat lighter and earlier, cut off screen time two hours before bed, stop hydrating and sip my tea two hours before bed, and slowly wind my mind and body down. Of course, having a regular lights-out bedtime window has been implemented as well. That's a lot to think about, but I'm worth it. My health and vitality are worth it. These are all things that I have control over for the most part.

Each day I practice these new intentions, I am investing in my well-being and creating more beneficial habits. As I do so, I am naturally releasing and replacing other mindless habits that do not support me. If I can improve by at least 1 percent, over time I will reap much more on my investment. As James Clear, author of *Atomic Habits,* states, "Small differences in performance can lead to very unequal distributions when repeated over time. This is yet another reason why habits are so important."

Consider one thing or one area in your life that you are willing to improve by 1 percent to set yourself up for a much greater return. What is it? Write it down. Implement the change today. You're worth it! Your health and vitality are worth it.

Stay Grounded

Intention: Anchored
Release: Others' energy

To hold space for others to feel the way they feel without being swept up in the energy requires one to stay grounded.

I became more aware of tense energy in our home this morning by noticing my own sensitivity. (Here, I thought that it was due to a long day yesterday, part of which included painting, and painting, and then more painting.) My son is in a funk, and I haven't been able to put my finger on what was going on with my partner. So, I shifted and grounded much of my own energy on the mat. Boy, am I grateful for my practice!

The morning routine with my son was challenging, but we made it through. Later, my partner confronted me about something that upset him. I was sideswiped by this, completely unaware of something important that had transpired between us earlier. There was clearly a non-verbal miscommunication.

I apologized for what I missed but was left feeling judged in a manner that was not representative of my character. We ended the brief conversation, agreeing that we will talk more later today. But I can't help but feel rocked.

We are not perfect. Others are not perfect. But when we know our relationships are anchored in love and respect, we hold space for people, including ourselves, to feel the way they feel, even when we may not agree. When emotions are heightened within and around, take a timeout to get grounded. Breathe, walk in nature, spend time on your mat, journal, and do what you need to anchor yourself.

COLLECTION 14

Purging

Clearing Trauma

Intention: Purge – Space for healing
Release: Unfounded beliefs

Tonight, the full moon's theme is about healing, and the full-moon event itself is a healing balm.

I've been on a sharp learning curve for the past few years. New business, new relationship, building a new house, new role as a caregiver, new lifestyle, and new season of womanhood (perimenopause). I'm grateful that I already have solid practices in place to stay present and grounded. Without them, I'd be a complete basket case. My nervous system would be in overdrive, and I would likely have other health issues.

Being alive is all it takes to accumulate trauma in the body. From small issues to those that turn life upside down, they find a home in the body unless we have a way to purge our system. Aside from daily practices like breathwork, meditation, movement, journaling, and nature, the full moon lends itself well to releasing the buildup.

Could you benefit from purging the lingering effects of your own trauma? I encourage you to create a habit of utilizing the energy of each full moon to support your healing. This will provide you with a regular monthly opportunity to clear out the accumulation.

Under the Radar

Intention: Purge – Space for possibilities
Release: What's run its course

Purging is the action of ridding or removing an unwanted quality, condition, or feeling.

There are the obvious and problematic somethings and someones in life that I have removed, or at the very least, I have created distance from. What I find more challenging is detecting the more subtle energies that don't shake me up too much. These behaviors, habits, or other clever manifestations fly mostly under my radar because they are so ingrained.

It's funny how reluctant I am to "see" this clutter when it comes to clearing out space for new possibilities. Most have served me well at some point in life, and I feel loyal to them. But alas, many old behaviors, habits, and beliefs have run their course. It's time to bag them and take them out to the street. If I need them again, I will upgrade to a version that is more compatible with who I am now.

The first thing I'm giving the heave-ho is every story others tell me or that I tell myself that paints me as a victim. There is no upgrade for this! It simply has to go!!

What is one something or someone that you would do well to purge? And what will you do with the extra space?

Damned Good Company

Intention: Purge – Space to be alone
Release: Overstimulation

We all need time alone. Spending regular, quality time with ourselves contributes to our overall wellness and supports autonomy.

Even as a young girl, I thoroughly enjoyed my time alone. Growing up in a large family, it could be a challenge to find unoccupied space. I learned that taking off on an adventure in the woods by our home, doggo by my side, I could explore and simply be without interruption. Nature, a bubble bath, and hanging out with our horses and barn cats were my retreats from the hubbub. I was very shy and insecure when I was young. I'm not certain why, but as a teenager, I overcompensated for this perceived weakness by staying very busy.

Busyness was also my go-to as a young adult. Being alone, still and quiet, felt like torture. As fate would have it, that was a rare occurrence being a single mother of four. Until I reached my 40s, I avoided time alone without other stimulation—TV, working, biking, running, or any activity that kept my mind occupied. I really thought moving my body was the only reason I was sane, as it distracted me from a life that felt incredibly overwhelming. And in hindsight, I acknowledge that it was indeed overwhelming.

While many of my coping mechanisms were quite healthy, their effects did not have longevity. I had to learn new strategies to calm my maxed-out nervous system. Yoga was and is my mainstay bundle of strategies. I spend the first forty-five to ninety minutes of my day breathing, chanting, meditating, and moving my body with intention.

Yoga is my space to be alone and present with myself, and it fills my cup. But even the best laid plans need to be tweaked now and again. I am craving more time alone. I feel my nervous system needs more moments of less stimulation, and with menopause on the horizon, I need more rest.

What do you feel in your body when you think about alone time? Do you feel tense or does your brain scream, "Hell, yeah!"? Get to know yourself by creating space and time to be alone. I'll bet you discover that you're damned good company, plus you will improve your overall health.

Be Silly

Intention: Purge – Space to play
Release: Adulting

Children remind us to stop taking life and ourselves so seriously!

I've been far too serious lately, neglecting my silly, playful inner child. My days have felt like a grind, and I'm worn out. Adulting can suck! I'm ready for a different approach to life. I realize that I cannot change the people around me or some of the present circumstances, but I sure as hell can change my outlook.

Today, I'll pick up my six-year-old grandson, and for the next couple of days I'm hanging out with him and my two-year-old granddaughter. They're the cool kids! Fun. Funny. Creative. Curious. Smart. Adventurous. Spontaneous. They live in the moment, seizing each with wide eyes and open minds. I plan to soak it all in and allow their vitality to cleanse and energize my soul. We'll play games, color, read, laugh, and be absolutely silly.

Do you need a break from adulting? Make a playdate with your children, grandchildren, nieces, nephews, random neighbor kids (just kidding on that last one), and have some good, clean fun! Leave the grown-up stuff to other adults for the day.

Priceless

Intention: Purge – More space to play
Release: Adulting

There's nothing quite like starting your day with giggles and pancakes.

Cooking pancakes with a six year old is good for the soul. The stove will need extra cleaning, but as Mastercard's ad campaign states, it's priceless. It's the things that money can't buy, like playing house inside of a giant box with my grandkids. Priceless!

For today, adulting is on the back burner and will have to wait until Monday. This space is for playing!

Can you rally for one more day of playing? Is it easy or difficult for you to release the culturally restrictive boundaries that define adulthood? Get curious about your answer. And lastly, consider how you can weave brevity into your life regularly. I bet you're a hoot! Don't be afraid to show your lighter side.

Gift of Change

Intention: Purge - Space to transition
Release: Attachment to what must change

Transitions are often overlooked as an essential space of their own. Here, we learn what is needed to move forward in the right direction.

With change being the one true consistency in life, it's crucial to engage in the space between what was and what is coming. In my experience, it's best to honor and respect transitions. They are a gift. In them we rest, heal, learn, gain strength, gather resources, and align our intentions with our hearts. It's a place and time to prepare for the next thing.

I have transitioned from childhood to adulthood, married to widowed, single to relationship, parenting small children to grandmother, employee to self-employed, menstruation to perimenopause, and much more. I have experienced continuous evolution from one state to the next. I am currently in a transition. It's a slow hand-off from the known to the unknown.

Living is about changing whether we want to or not. Digging our heels in and fighting against it will only wear us out. Rushing ahead will leave us unprepared. Transitions connect the past and future.

When we reach the end of a transition, we are instinctively aware it's time to move forward and are likely aligned in the direction of our next steps. Embracing change is a learned behavior that builds resilience, meaning we release the old more quickly, hold space for the transition, and are excited when it's time to step into the unknown.

Many people love change while others resist. How do you feel about change? If that term makes you cringe, does it feel better to think about these inevitable nudges and shifts as transitions, evolution, or transformation? Sit with your eyes closed, taking five to ten full belly breaths and notice the bodily sensations and mental stirrings that arise as you consider each term (change, transition, evolution, and transformation). Now, create an affirmation using the word that resonates with you.

Landing Safely

Intention: Purge – Space for the unknown
Release: Fear of the unknown

"Fear not the unknown. It is a sea of possibilities."

—Tom Althouse

Even calculated risks are based on unverifiable factors. That's why it's scary! I do prefer a slowly unfolding mystery over being thrown from a plane and only having the falling time to ponder what's next. Having time to consider possible outcomes gives me a feeling of having some control mixed with the excitement of what will flow to me over the sea of possibility.

For some time, I've had a taste of both the out-of-nowhere unknown and the drawn-out "where the hell is this going?" unknown. The latter is where I am struggling. It feels like falling from a plane without a parachute, but I can't see the ground yet. As much as I want to completely release the need to know where and how I'll land, I'm still grasping for answers.

What I'm imagining is scary, and these thoughts steal my energy. Have I been through the worst of this storm? Will it get easier? Will life ever feel "normal" again? Is this the new normal? My temporary solution is to hold space for and find peace in what is unknown, such as answers to these questions, what tomorrow holds, and where I'll land.

Maybe you have a situation that is a whole bag of scary mysteries. A loved one's health, your health, finances, a relationship, or a career are just a few possibilities. Together, let's purge the clutter of fear and leave space for what is currently unknown to unfold in its time. The present solution is to lean on one another and trust that we will land safely.

Meditation

Intention: Purge – Space for contemplation
Release: Restrictions (hidden areas)

Stillness and quiet can be wonderful companions for contemplating life.

When I first started my meditation practice, it felt like torture. Being still was challenging for my body, and being quiet was more of a noisy chaos. I struggled to be with myself because I had been living in a chronic state of stress for years. My nervous system was in a constant state of vigilance, and I was feeling the results as anxiety and dis-ease. I stuck it out, determined to figure out for myself what others (and science) had discovered as a path to peace and healing.

I started meditating (if you could call it that) for five minutes each day. I set a timer so I wouldn't keep opening one eye to check the time. Over the weeks, I learned to be more still and accepted that my mind would often drift. As the months passed, I was able to find more stillness and eventually worked up to meditating for twenty to thirty minutes. I discovered new tools to gently bring my mind back to the present, mainly my breath and feeling into the earth beneath me. These techniques spilled over into many parts of my life, and I could feel my entire being shift to a more healthy and peaceful state.

These days, I'm able to explore areas of my mind and life without hiding what I don't particularly like. I still feel a twinge of guilt, shame, or regret as I cross into parts that my inner security team had previously taped off, but my time in contemplation *has been* and *is* healing my mind and body.

If you currently have a meditation practice, continue to deepen it. If you haven't tried it or you have and it felt like torture, try a walking meditation to begin. Take a mindful walk in nature, tuning into the colors or sounds. To begin a seated meditation practice, try using a timer, beginning with five minutes. Here, focus on your breath and the earth beneath you.

Time and Seasons

Intention: Purge – Space for right the timing
Release: Forcing

"Everything on earth has its own time and its own season."[6]

(Ecclesiastes 3:1 CEV)

The timing of when things happen is often a mystery to me. What I do know is that life plays out on a timeline that I don't control, and if I'm wise, I don't try to control it. Don't get me wrong, there are occasions that I want to and have forced pieces into place. The results weren't what I had hoped. Timing is not something to whack over the head with a stick and drag into the lair of personal expectations.

I am half planner and half spontaneous action. I used to be more rigid with planning but discovered a trick I used to call "the wing-it method." Today, we fondly call it MSU (Making Shit Up). Now, I know this open approach is about being in the flow of life.

MSU is an awareness of when to move based on a state of present-mindedness. It's a connection with the internal and external that triggers when to act and apply our accumulation of experience, knowledge, gifts, and skills. MSU isn't exactly an accurate description. It's just a fun expression to describe an organic response to living in the moment that is possible by having prepared throughout life.

What is your relationship with timing? If you are inclined to force the puzzle pieces of life together, would you be willing to open yourself to holding space for the right timing? Find a quiet place to contemplate a specific issue you are struggling with, and when you are settled, listen to your heart. And remember that everything has its own time and season.

A Beginner's Mind

Intention: Purge – Space for curiosity & self-discovery
Release: Judgment

Being curious requires openness, humility, and a sense of adventure.

On the lighter side, curiosity can be playful. There's also a need for us to dig deep into all our mental and emotional corners. This is best done with an inquisitive and pure, even childlike mind.

When I first began the practice of being curious about my own behaviors and beliefs, it was scary. On the sidelines of my vulnerability was my inner critic, yelling out judgments. She was ruthless. As much as I wanted to retreat and stop asking questions, I stayed the course and learned so much about myself. Parts were difficult to take in, and I knew I had my work cut out to become the woman I wanted to be.

The adventure of self-discovery was a steep climb in the beginning. But as I forged forward, the heckling voice of judgment became muffled and faint. This is not to say that I'm always secure and confident, but I know the path forward is to stand firm in my attributes as well as my imperfections. Taking time to be with and see myself as I am has been, hands down, the best and most challenging of times.

This probing, questioning, and clearing out the dark corners to know the self is a lifetime process and one that results in more joy, more contentment, better health, better relationships, and a deeper clarity of purpose.

How well do you know yourself? Do you ever question your behaviors and beliefs? Can you look at yourself with love and acceptance? If you answered "no" to any of these questions, then it's time to step onto the path of self-discovery.

Be Yourself

Intention: Purge – Space for expression
Release: Being reserved

Express yourself every day in your own unique way.

We each have our own distinct way of moving through life. How we dress, speak, move, work, and play reveals who we are. Have you heard the saying, "Be yourself, everyone else is taken?" That's it! So, if you love to sing, sing. If you are moved to dance, dance. Purge what no longer resonates with you and make space to express in your own beautiful ways.

COLLECTION 15

Improving

Worry

Intention: Improve self-care
Release: Worrying

Stress has a way of depleting energy. It taxes every system in the body and when stretched out over time, it can be the catalyst for disease.

Knowing the ultimate outcome of chronic stress makes taking time for self-care absolutely essential. I'm motivated and committed to taking better care of myself. But I'm sticking to the rule of 1 percent because I know from experience how small changes lead to grand and lasting results.

When I was a young adult, I remember telling my grandma that she worried enough for the whole family. In fact, I said that she worried enough that no one else needed to bother. Flash forward thirty years and here I am, worrying. Today, I'm going to set up a worry jar and give these stress-inducing thought nuggets a place to dwell besides my mind and body. Most of what we dread never happens anyway, so worry really is a waste of resources.

If you are a worrier or the "family worrier," why not make a worry jar? It will be a great exercise to help you become more aware of what's bumping around in your mind—and get it out! Give it a try. It's a simple way to take better care of yourself.

Amnesia

Intention: Improve self-care
Release: Long-held tension

Part of what I've noticed that adds to my low energy is muscle tension. My neck and shoulders are taut and have been for as long as I can remember.

I've been very active all of my life, and I still love to go hard. But as much as I love it, I've had to change how I think about movement. Recently, I learned more about somatics and how these gentle, intentional movements help heal muscles by allowing them to release fully. My life, like so many others, has been pretty stressful, especially because I already experience anxiety.

My shoulders climb up toward my ears when I'm stressed, and over the years, I lost my awareness of this. The result is that I am left with contracted muscles, even when I'm relaxed. This is called SMA—Sensory Motor Amnesia.

I'm excited to begin the journey of healing my shoulders through somatic movements and letting go of the long-held tension. The body awareness I've learned through my yoga practice has guided me to this point. I'm listening to and trusting my body. It's not that I can no longer "go hard," but that I will do it more mindfully.

Our bodies are amazingly intelligent, strong, resilient, and able to heal if we give them what they need. What does your body need? Are you listening? What is one way you can improve self-care?

Getting There

Intention: Improve self-care
Release: Rushing

"We'll get there when we f@*king get there!"

I was really looking forward to resuming sibling breakfast time at a local greasy spoon café. When our regular meeting space closed, we stopped our weekly get-togethers. We started gathering once again when a new business opened, and then life happened, and we were off once again. Today, we're gathering for a late breakfast.

The morning routine with my son takes as long as it takes. There's no rushing. We progressed through the process and finished in good time. My sweetheart had the truck running as I worked toward making myself presentable for being in public. I haven't had a very high standard for this lately, but I needed a few minutes. And then, I started to feel rushed and irritated. (This was all in my head, mind you.) That is when I made the above statement. It wasn't one of my finer moments, but stating this to myself had a wonderful way of reducing the pressure.

When we are doing all we can but still feel pressed and rushed, it's time to pause and breathe. There you go! You have two simple tools to improve self-care. You'll get there when you get there! And an occasional expletive doesn't hurt either. The point is to let go of the tension, get out there, and enjoy the amazing people in your life. Have fun!

Breathe Deeply

Intention: Improve self-care
Release: Feeling pressured

The feeling of being under pressure triggers the stress response, bringing all bodily systems on high alert.

Mostly, I think that I stress myself out with a busy mind. Overthinking, although I'm not as good at it as I used to be, is still an issue for me. Yes, there are instances where I feel pressure from others that is real, but more often, it comes from within. I understand how strenuous stress is on my body, yet I still fall into this trap. When I catch myself, I close my eyes (unless I'm driving), take several deep breaths, and sigh them out. This brings me back into my parasympathetic nervous system, restoring calm and shifting my ability to reason back online.

For the most part, situations and events in life turn out just fine. Of course, there are occasions when they don't. Deep breathing is a response that benefits us either way. We literally cannot think straight when we're in the stress response, and this only exacerbates the issue at hand. Why not start the practice of deep breathing when you feel pressured?

Never Too Late

Intention: Improve self-care
Release: Perfectionism

It's easy to believe that we will never get our shit together and may as well give up on making positive lifestyle changes—especially when we're older and our hair has turned gray. What's the point?!

I can't help but remember when a woman in her 70s asked me if it was too late for her to heal and change. It hit me hard, and I couldn't respond fast enough with, "Absolutely not!"

It isn't often enough that I give myself credit for small but steady strides in the right direction. It's more likely that I'll catch my slips and failures. If I had a friend that treated me that way, we would have a conversation. Today, I'm going to monitor my inner voice. For every criticism, she will need to come up with three compliments. In other words, she will need to catch me doing something right—even by her lofty standards! She will have to pay close attention to notice and acknowledge each small stride I make that contributes to positive change.

Making lifestyle changes can be challenging. Change is not an all-or-nothing effort—either we get it right, or we give up. Real change is an accumulation of small successes peppered with slips and failures. No one is perfect. If your inner voice refuses anything but perfection, let her know that she will owe you three kudos for every criticism. Be sure to write these compliments in your journal for future encouragement.

In the Trenches

Intention: Focus on the good
Release: Negativity

The mantra I share weekly on SM and via email is taken from Tanaaz Chubb's book *My Pocket Mantras*. This week's mantra is "I focus on all the things that are good in my life."[7]

This mantra brings to mind the negativity bias. It's human nature to be more psychologically impacted by negative events than positive events, even when the magnitude of both are equal. This fact is based on research.

I know I'm up against an innate quality. I also know from experience that allowing myself to walk too close to the mental edge of negativity is a very slippery slope. It's like a fly getting too close to the car window you have nicely cracked for him. Zoop! He's sucked into oblivion in the blink of an eye. Negativity has the power to do the same with the mind and is not something to be trifled with.

Life events are a mixed bag of good, bad, and everything in between that is categorized by our individual perceptions. The key is to be aware of our mental focus. When annoying, negative thoughts are buzzing around your head, immediately crack the window and let them be sucked out into the ether.

While your desire may be to focus on what seems good, which is awesome, you will still be enticed by negativity. So, when you're being squeezed, remember that both "good" and "bad" events are temporary in nature. Nothing stays the same, thus allowing each to run its course. There is likely a silver lining to be found, even in the trenches.

Listen

Intention: "Be skeptical, but learn to listen"—Don Miguel Ruiz, and Janet Mills, *The Fifth Agreement*[8]
Release: Self-sabotage

It's a wonderful surprise when something positive happens, especially when we didn't really believe it would.

Skepticism is a very smart practice and a key to learning. It requires critical thinking—inquiry, open-mindedness, and a willingness to bump up against the status quo. Through the course of gathering more information, we either build a case for belief or disbelief or decide there's not enough to support either. This approach can apply to life both internally and externally.

A cynic is quite different from a skeptic, as a cynic refuses to believe in or trust what is right in front of them. It shows up when making a determination or judgment before having a reasonable understanding. The "truth" is decided without investigating or seeking further clarity. There are sources in our real and virtual worlds that are hell-bent on selling us their snake oil through manipulation and deceit. Some are subtle, while others are outright belligerent. We come by cynicism honestly and of course, have every right to protect ourselves.

Unfortunately, we can also be deceived by our own thoughts. This is how we may sabotage our hopes and dreams. It's important to question personal beliefs and behaviors and to be skeptical in a loving and compassionate way.

If you take time to listen to your inner dialogue, you may discover, in small or not-so-small ways, you have been deceived. Be a dear and kind friend to yourself, but don't hesitate to ask yourself the tough questions. And then, be skeptical, but learn to listen.

Swearing May Help

Intention: Easy f*@cking flow
Release: Tension

My biggest trial in life has always been my mind. So far, one of my greatest successes has been changing the way I think. Looking back on my 40s, I see how far I've come. When I look ahead to the remainder of my 50s, I'm excited to continue the rewiring project of my nervous system.

I have a sign in my yoga room that says, "Maybe swearing will help." While there may be people who are offended, I personally appreciate the zing of a well-placed expletive. It's like a turbo kicking in to boost a statement. Today, that turbo is boosting my intention to a higher level. Each time I fall out of my flow because my thoughts are jacked up, my shoulder muscles contract. That's my cue to repeat my intention while taking a deep breath in and sighing the tension out.

If your muscles are tense and your mind unruly today, you'll need something to boost you back into an easy f*@cking flow. Maybe swearing will help.

Treasure

Intention: Fierce serenity
Release: Not trusting

Standing in your power when the ground is shifting under your feet is not only possible but has the power to change the outcome of your current experience.

Most of what rocks our boats are gentle waves. Life is so much more peaceful when we let go of the small stuff. The disruptions of major life events usually land atop an accumulation of small stuff, which can make minor events feel large and grand events grander. The result is overwhelm, a.k.a. stress. So, how do we even begin to work through it all? It's the same approach to eating an elephant—one bite at a time.

In this scenario, we have the opportunity to become a sculptor. We can chip away at the giant mound with creativity and intention and with ferocity. We can trust that what seems like rubble holds a treasure. After the time and effort of carving and sorting, there comes a day that we discover that underneath the pile of big and small events is an indomitable, fiercely serene warrior. Through this process, we can see our true strength through trusting eyes.

What image comes to mind when you read the following words? Strength, a quiet force, grounded calmness, gentle soul, and peaceful warrior. Today, stand in your power, be fierce with serenity and let the image you see be you. You are all of this and so much more!

Belief

Intention: Expectations
Release: Expectations

To have expectations or not have expectations, that is the question.

Ex·pec·ta·tion: a strong belief that something will happen or be the case in the future

In my thinking, expectations come quite naturally. In fact, it's nearly impossible not to have them. There are times when I have been thoroughly disappointed by making predictions about events and about people. This has started me on a path to ditch assumptions altogether. Why not just take outcomes and people as they come and save the energy?

I've been working on healing my tense and sore shoulders and neck. In this case, I have not made a solid commitment to the outcome, and this is a problem. I want to heal, but I'm tentative about believing that I will be successful. I don't necessarily have that expectation.

These are two different views on expectations. In the first, it seems I'm better off leaving the future to work itself out, and in the second, my belief that I will heal is paramount to the healing process. Really, expectations are a mix of experience and a hopeful belief when positive. In the negative, they are a combination of experience and doubt. It would seem that having expectations weighs heavily on how things turn out because we influence the turn of events with the power of our thoughts.

Your thoughts hold great power! Your expectations influence every aspect of life. Do your best to manage them. With mindful awareness, you can harness the upside of either having or not having expectations depending on the situation.

COLLECTION 16

Living

Healing in Time

Intention: Trust the process
Release: Timeframe

It takes far less time to heal than it does to cause the injury in the first place. April fools!

I wish it were true, but healing takes time. In a culture of instant gratification, trusting in a process that has no solid completion date is a test of patience. Even so, I find it easier to accept. For me, the process is where I learn and grow into the person that can embody the outcome.

The goals and dreams I have waited for and worked at over time have morphed and transitioned parallel to my own transformation. In the end, they turned out much richer and more fulfilling than I envisioned. In my experience, quick and easy are lousy ways to learn and obtain anything valuable.

So today, I will do the work and hold space for the universe to breathe and conspire for my greatest good. I will put one foot in front of the other, stay present, be open to growth, and invite the magic of the process to swirl within and around me.

Have you all but given up on healing from an injury whether physical or emotional? I encourage you to practice patience by taking one step and day at a time. Do the work. Trust that the process will transform you within the perfect timeframe. Afterall, the universe is conspiring for your greatest good.

This is Hard

Intention: Compassion
Release: Feeling f*cked

Having self-compassion puts me in a state of being to show compassion more completely to others.

Days have accumulated into weeks and weeks into months. In less than three months, we will be at the one-year anniversary of my son's crash. Parts of the experience have been like a nightmare, but mostly it has been a long and very daily challenge. I have noticed a cycle that begins with a slow decline into depression, anger, and deeper depression that leads to shutting down. The silence is in stark contrast to the outbursts of frustration.

After days, maybe a week, a lightness begins to emerge. It's palpable when I enter his room. In the days before this break, it was hard to move through the door, and I tensed after speaking, unsure if my words would bring more silence or a sharp response.

I've noticed that the cycle has shifted somewhat. The periods of complete withdrawal are shorter, leaving more space for engagement, real conversation, and compassion. My partner told me that it's okay to say that this is hard, but I'm resisting for fear that I will start to believe it and energize it.

I want the opposite! I want to feel free and light, flowing through the days without feeling like I'm wearing lead boots. The reality is that it's NOT easy! At times I feel trapped, weary, and then guilty for feeling f*cked.

I'm ready to really show myself much-needed compassion. I'm going to let my guard down and allow space for the grief I feel to make its way out through crying or anger sessions, writing, moving my body, and whatever else is healthy and moves this energy. I want to see myself fully. By holding space for self-compassion, I believe my compassion for my son and others will reach a deeper level.

Are you in the midst of difficulties right now? Do you feel the heaviness of grief? First, show yourself deep compassion by allowing yourself to feel your emotions without judgment. And it's okay to say it's hard.

Letting Off Steam

Intention: Pay attention
Release: What I cannot control

It is a profound revelation when we realize that we are in control of very little in life, but what is in our control is the most important aspect.

One area of life I have learned to feel quite confident about is that I'm responsible for my own behavior. I'm responsible for my choices, my words, and how I respond to life. You may be thinking this is an obvious role of any adult, and I agree. Gone are the days of expressing our disapproval with a temper tantrum. Too bad, as it's a great way to move the energy of frustration and anger out of the body.

My experience as an adult is that we have moved on from kicking and screaming but have replaced that behavior with more crafty and subtle responses to express our disapproval. Here are a few that I may or may not have tried myself: being passive-aggressive, manipulating, ignoring, eating too much, not eating, shopping, blaming, punishing, binging movies, and avoiding.

I'm certain there are plenty more, but this list will suffice to make the point that we only learn to own our behavior by doing so intentionally. It requires our attention, and without being mindful, we likely respond with a mindless tantrum each time things don't go our way.

There are times when shit goes sideways, and it would feel so good to kick and scream to get my way, but alas, my behavior is the one solid thing I can control. This is not to say that letting off some steam is irresponsible.

There are occasions when "letting the badger out" can relieve the rising internal tension caused by what I cannot control. In this case, I vent. I move my body, journal, yell in the woods (sorry, critters!), swear, express my disapproval directly, etc. I do my best to get it out without damaging others, but I have to pay attention and be honest with myself.

How do you respond to things you cannot control? Do you have some healthy and effective tools to let the steam off?

Flexible

Intention: Honor time (none is wasted)
Release: Timing

Have you ever said, "I don't have time for this!"?

I find it curious that time is a social construct. In fact, it wasn't until 1883 that the railroad adopted the national standardized time format to synchronize their operations. Many citizens were not in favor of a standard time system, especially since the government was forcing it on them. One newspaper headline back then stated, "Let the people of Cincinnati stick to the truth as it is written by the sun, moon and stars."[9]

I have certainly claimed to not have time. "I'm too busy" and "I don't have time" are statements we all use. The fact is we all have the same amount of time each day. Just because we may not accomplish what we had hoped due to having our well-made plans altered or even derailed, our allotment is still twenty-four hours. And just because what popped up is not on our list, our time is not wasted.

Of course, we can't allow all our plans to be disrupted, but we can certainly be more flexible. The problem with being too rigid with our time is that we can force our agenda and miss the right timing, not to mention stress ourselves out. The problem with thinking that we've wasted our day is that we blind ourselves to the beauty of synchronicity.

At the end of today, take time to reflect back on how often your plans or schedule were interrupted. What was happening in those moments that your time was "wasted?" Is it possible that you were blessed with the perfect timing of the sun, moon, and stars? How can you honor time by being more flexible?

Hold Space

Intention: Carry on
Release: Yesterday's energy

Have you ever felt like suicide was an option to relieve your emotional pain?

I have definitely been there. My most intense experience was in December 2015. It was three months after I ended a very long-term relationship and almost two months after my mother finally succumbed to cancer. I was home alone around Christmas time as the kids were on a road trip to Florida with cousins. The accumulation of stress had reached an all-time high, and I wanted a way out.

The irony is that I was working as a Certified Prevention Specialist. One of my major areas of focus was suicide. My firsthand experience with feeling completely without hope equipped me with a profound empathy for other people suffering to the point that suicide seems a reasonable choice—or the only answer.

So far, we have had two events of being on the ledge with my son since we arrived home from the hospital. He's lost so much and struggles daily with physical, emotional, and mental pain. But knowing I could walk out of the room having seen him alive for the last time, sucks. It sucks so much that I cannot accurately describe it. It's a thorough wrenching of the mind, body, emotions, and soul to simply hold space for the suffering and for the possibility.

Today, the heavy darkness has lifted, and we are here to carry on. In 2015, I wrestled with myself all night and finally decided that I wanted to live. This was my turning point and the beginning of my healing journey, the one that led me to starting my business to help other women. I didn't know that it would also equip me to support my own son in his darkest days. But as I stated, today we're off the ledge, and yesterday's energy must be released. Healing must begin anew.

Don't fear yourself or others who are suicidal. Hold space. Be present with love and acceptance. Dig deep. Reach out. Your experience with darkness has meaning and a grand purpose that may not be apparent at present but will be revealed at just the right time. For now, carry on.

Breath of Joy

Intention: Alchemy
Release: Any resistance to shift

The art and magic of transforming a problem into an asset, a negative into a positive, and a fear into a strength—that's alchemy.

The truth is that while I've bounced back into daily rituals, my body and mind still hold the experience of trauma. I've had a relentless pain in my right shoulder blade and substantial tension in my entire right side since the frightening event with my son. I gave myself extra care yesterday, as I will today, to gently work through and transform the mental and emotional pain that is manifesting physically.

In addition, I have been resistant to changing my business focus. Even now, I'm not quite sure if it's the right time. Before I left my employer, I wanted to support women by helping them heal themselves from the cuts and bruises of life. While this is still true, I've heard a subtle inner voice telling me that it's time to shift my approach. I just don't have a vision for this new and unknown direction, which is scary.

What I do know is that magic happens in transitions. It begins first with inner transformation, which is the catalyst for growth and inevitably leads to the conception, development, and birth of new ideas and purpose. Like any pregnancy and birth, there are pains and fear in the process. For now, I will settle into the discomfort and simply trust. I'll do my best to stay open until the time comes for the shifting to bring forth what is next.

Is there something you do daily to practice transitioning? I highly recommend yoga as an effective practice of alchemy. You can use any aspect of yoga as a tool to shift from one state of body and mind to another. Give the following a try. It's called Breath of Joy and is popular in my classes because it's invigorating for the body and mind because it catalyzes shift.

Stand with your feet hip distance apart. Breathe in through your nose while raising your arms shoulder height, palms down to the front, then lower them. Take another breath in while raising your arms shoulder height, palms down to the sides, then lower. Take a third inhale while raising your arms above your head, palms forward. Exhale with a powerful HA! as you bend forward while lowering your arms down to the sides of your legs. Return to standing upright and repeat vigorously five to ten times.

Acknowledge

Intention: Celebrate
Release: Yes, release

Birthdays are an opportunity to acknowledge our arrival into the physical realm and our unique and essential role in the universe.

Today is my son's 25th birthday. Earlier this week, I wasn't sure he'd be living and that we'd be celebrating with him. But the sun is shining, spring is in the air, and I'm soaking in the sound of his voice coming from the other room. He is in the midst of stories being shared by my daughter and her boyfriend. The bullshit is flying, and I couldn't be more content.

My two-year-old granddaughter and I whipped up a cake earlier. The sweet smell from the oven has permeated the kitchen. We will be celebrating and are extra grateful that we have the opportunity to do so. We will celebrate more time together, the creation of more memories, and the resilience of family bonds under very tough circumstances.

Birthdays are important and, in my opinion, always worth acknowledging in a special way. You are the only you. You have a special role and essential place in the world—in the universe. Celebrate yourself. Celebrate those you love most. Celebrate those who are alone. We are stronger together, and there is no guarantee of when we will celebrate our final birthday. So, release all else and celebrate!

What a Ride

Intention: Regular maintenance
Release: Rickety parts

"Life should not be a journey to the grave with the intention of arriving safely in a pretty and well preserved body, but rather to skid in broadside in a cloud of smoke, thoroughly used up, totally worn out, and loudly proclaiming "Wow! What a Ride!"

—Hunter S. Thompson, *The Proud Highway: Saga of a Desperate Southern Gentleman, 1955-1967*[10]

This quote has long inspired me. Do I live this way? Not really. But I believe there is a way to live life to the fullest and care for yourself. I liken this idea to mountain biking, which is an activity that takes all I have and pushes me beyond what I know I'm capable of.

I'm exhilarated after I ride, but my bike and body recover well only when I practice regular maintenance. I nourish, hydrate, and stretch my body. I clean and oil the bike chain, wash the dust and/or mud off, check the tires, and tighten parts as needed. This sets me up for the next ride.

Taking risks and having an incredible ride does not have to leave us drained and used up. It's also true that a great life cannot be accomplished without taking risks. We do well by putting energy into our dreams and giving them our all, and when we need to recharge, we roll into the garage, park, and break out the tools. The grand ride is a lifetime of great rides strung together with as many recoveries and maintenance stops as we need to prepare for the next leg of the journey.

Where are you on the spectrum of playing it safe and skidding along life in a cloud of smoke? Are you in need of recovery and maintenance or could you push and challenge yourself more? Answer these questions in your journal and include one thing you will do today to contribute to a lifetime theme of "Wow! What a Ride!"

Spring

Intention: Welcome & embrace the new day
Release: Dark days

Winter leaves Wyoming on its own terms! It coexists with spring until it finally retires temporarily.

You would be hard pressed to find one person in Wyoming at this point in the year who wants to see even one more snowflake. We all desire to have the icy wind replaced with a cool breeze and the dark, cloud-covered sky replaced with deep blue and sunshine. Seeing patches of brown grass gives hope that the mounds of snow will give way to green—something we have not seen for months! Spring is welcomed with open arms and much gratitude.

Personally, I am also welcoming brighter days emotionally and mentally. I give myself credit for surviving the long, dark nights of the winter season and another winter of my soul. The longer days and melting snow make me feel hopeful. I can feel the layers of heaviness melting away from deep within.

Maybe you are making your way through a dark time. I encourage you to acknowledge yourself for taking every difficult step. Do so by writing in your journal and/or creating an affirmation that reflects your strength and resilience. And when the new day or season arrives, welcome it with a warm embrace.

Processing Life

Intention: Solid foundation
Release: Myself

How we process life impacts our health more than what happens in life.

I finally went to my chiropractor today. I've been practicing somatic exercises for the past three weeks with the intention of healing the tight muscles in my shoulders and back. Somatics is a way to retrain the brain to fully release muscles that have remained partly contracted due to stress (mental, emotional, and physical) and restore their full function. At some point, I stopped noticing my muscles were tight. But I have been reminded over the past few years because of how my yoga practice reconnects my mind and body.

As I have learned to calm my nervous system, I have become more fully aware of my thoughts and physiology. I have learned so much about myself through this process of releasing layer after layer of built-up stress. Although I thought I was ready for the next step, my body informed me that I must first establish a solid foundation. The full function of my muscles comes after the structure to which they are attached is secure and aligned.

My advice? Learn healthy ways that support you with letting go of the problems and pressures of life sooner rather than later. This will give you a solid foundation and as you release the external tension, you will gain the extra benefit of releasing the internal (a.k.a. yourself).

COLLECTION 17

Discovering

Decisions

Intention: Intuition
Release: Spinning

There are times when decision-making is a stressful, roundabout process for me.

Teetering between two choices can be nerve-racking if I'm stuck on the spin cycle. Sometimes, I forget that I'm fully capable of making great decisions, and I have made some great ones in my life. The hesitation is based on the not-so-stellar selections that are also on my resumé. But at this point, I'd rather make a just okay choice over sitting on the fence spinning away. Besides, one can only teeter on the fence so long before a decision is made without them.

We all have intuition. Do you know that gut feeling that tells us yes, no, not now, more information is needed, and so on? The trick is that we must be connected to our whole being—mind, body, emotions, and spirit. The nervous system is the key to picking up subtle clues which is why it is best to proceed from a grounded and stable place. A spinning mind is a perpetual ride in the stress response, which does not lend itself to reason, plus it jams our intuition.

Today, set aside space and time to listen to your body. If you need to make a decision, whether small, medium, or large, sit with your options and trust that your intuition will guide you.

Sigh of Relief

Intention: Just do it
Release: Procrastination

I admire people who get the jump on tasks and projects they don't particularly like.

Things that take extra time, have a missing piece, or just don't bring me any joy, get put on the back burner. I can procrastinate with the best! I can find untold distractions to distance myself from the doldrums of what I find boring and egregious. But today, I am committed. I will complete two projects that I will find joy only in knowing they are complete: taxes and warranty paperwork (big sigh).

Do you have something hanging over your head that needs your attention? Today, commit to a date and time to tackle one task or project that has been on your procrastination list. If you can do it today, that's even better! If not, when that tedious or arduous task pops up on your calendar, go after it like a defensive tackle in the Super Bowl! You will likely feel a bit lighter and let out a big sigh of relief.

Grief

Intention: Be present & feel
Release: Covering up

Yesterday, the dark clouds rolled in, and I knew I should stop trying to escape.

I give myself credit for coming through some deep shit and embracing life with joy on the other side. I've resisted slipping through the crack in the door to immerse myself in the dark. I resisted until there were too many pieces stacked up, like a game of Jenga, and I was afraid they would all fall at once.

I decided it would be better to surrender early before losing my resolve altogether. My emotions were building up, and it felt imperative to withdraw, cry, and sit with them. I took a good look at them, acknowledged them, and accepted that they were as normal as anyone may have under the circumstances.

Grief is crafty, and experiencing it deeply feels like shit. For me, it feels like anger, frustration, sadness, and at times, all-consuming. Yet, being present with such emotions and openly moving through them is the path to healing. I know this. It really doesn't matter what anyone else thinks.

Here are a few things I've done today to move through my grief:

- Sobbing as I lay on the side of the road sprawled out (mountain road, no traffic)
- Declining lunch with a friend and not forcing myself to be okay
- Not filling in or pouring energy into conversations I'm not ready to have

- Sticking to my morning practice, keeping it simple
- Walking in nature
- Taking a hot bath
- Letting it all hang out by not covering up how I feel

When you are going through a dark night of the soul, please be kind to yourself. Give yourself what you intuitively know you need. Don't feel obligated to carry on as if you're okay. Those who don't hold space for you to grieve and to feel are not looking out for your best interests. Some things take time and require you to focus on yourself. This is one of them.

Are you carrying grief? Whether it is from long ago or fresh, please know it's okay to not be okay. Give yourself what you need to grieve and heal.

The Work of Warriors

Intention: Gentle recovery
Release: Dark energy

The business of moving through heavy emotions takes a lot of energy.

Today, I awoke feeling lighter and more rested. What a relief! Yesterday was a workout for my mind, body, emotions, and soul. Even though I'm feeling much better, I need a down day to start recovering from the purging process. I've enjoyed a gentle yoga practice and spent extra time journaling about the experience to continue flushing out more of the dark energy. I feel tender and more spacious. I feel grateful, loved, and supported.

Sitting with grief and all of the emotions associated with grief is challenging, but it's also courageous. Facing fears and seeing yourself fully and exactly as you are is the work of warriors. Know that you have everything you need and are deserving of a gentle recovery after the battle.

Speak to Your Soul

Intention: Write it & release it
Release: Dark energy, frustration

Journaling is where I speak with my soul and leave my troubles.

I've been on a mission for several years to free myself from the clutches of anxiety. Although I'm tempted to think the previous few days of darkness were a setback, intuitively, I know they are an important part of my journey toward healing.

Yes, I am in a difficult season of life, and that is frustrating. I have lost much and hold space for my son's suffering daily. Yes, it's a possibility that I may lose him at a young age. I'm in this for the long run, and I have to find balance and peace to support my health.

But I can argue that I have also gained a lot. I am more capable of being with others as they fight their own battles and hold space for their grief. I have better awareness of my own field of energy and emotions—what is mine and what belongs to someone else.

I use journaling as a place to release what is not mine and process what is. I vent, swear, celebrate, criticize, and unload my burdens through writing rather than dumping unnecessarily on those I love. It's not that I don't keep those lines of communication open, but often, my writing is the best way to understand my own inner workings.

If you don't currently journal, it's time to start. Write and release. Free yourself of old and new frustrations and emotions. We all have them, and we all deserve to live a life of balance and ease.

Peace & Answers

Intention: Pause & ask
Release: Uncertainty

Learning to be okay with not knowing is an art of the peaceful soul.

If I'm honest, I don't know more than I do know. It's not that I don't seek knowledge or truth or hold space for possibilities. I do. But I've learned that most decisions I make are based on what I think I know. The more times I am rewarded with a good outcome, the more confident and at ease I am when faced with the next choice. When the results are so-so or not great, I file what I have learned from the mediocre outcome. Even so, it can be discouraging when things don't turn out like I hope.

Really, though, there's more to it than that. I am rediscovering the power of the pause. Pausing to sit with decisions and asking, "What does my soul have to say about it?" is a practice I have known but that I've let slip away. I can gather all the information and review it cognitively, but until I stop and check in with my heart and soul, I have not tapped into all my resources. It's definitely time to reinstate this beautiful practice of tuning into my deepest, truest, most wise self. Even when an obvious answer does not come right away, there is a silent knowing, an intuitive nudge of how to proceed.

When was the last time you paused to ask your soul's input on an important decision … or on any decision? This simple practice will draw you inward, where you will find peace and, when the time is right, *answers*.

Strength in Letting Go

Intention: Make wise changes
Release: Holding

"Some of us think holding on makes us strong; but sometimes it is letting go."

—Hermann Hesse

At heart, I am someone who holds on. I have shirts that are twenty years old and have lived in the same home for twenty-seven years. I have held on too long to jobs, relationships, shoes, and more. I've always seen this aspect of me as loyal, but to be honest, also fearful. Change can be scary, but it's also inevitable. It's a matter of changing on my own terms or letting life roll over me.

Being the initiator of change takes courage, energy, commitment, and self-discipline. I find that I have to dig deep for these assets as of late. I question if I have what it takes to see my goals through. I question the timing. I question my own abilities. What I do not question is that I must make changes—wise changes that align me with my dreams.

We all have a stance in regard to change. Some people dig in their heels, fold their arms, and refuse it, while others excitedly grab its hand and skip off into the sunset. But for most of us, it just depends on what the change entails. Realistically, change is a constant whether we initiate, embrace, or resist it.

Today, sit with your heart and soul and tap into your inner wisdom. Do your best to be present as a seeker and observer, allowing what has run its course to be set free and marvel at the strength of letting go. As you sit, bring your hands into ksepana mudra by drawing your palms together and interlacing all but your pointer fingers. Press your pointer fingers together and cross your thumbs. Now, point toward the ground. Breathe and release.

Clearing

Intention: Tune in
Release: Clatter

By tuning into our own unique rhythm, we tap our superpower of discernment.

I have given externalities far too much of my time and attention over the years. Often, these distractions are what I have preferred over listening to the constant dialogue in my head. I didn't understand back then (in my twenties and thirties) that I could change the content and tone of my inner voice. So, not only was there a clatter in the world around me, but there was also a constant clatter in my head. No wonder my nervous system was so jacked up!

Fast forward to a fifty-five-year-old me. I honestly have a pretty quiet and clear mind. I will give aging a little credit, but mostly it's the result of finding and applying new ways of being. Some seemed a bit strange at first, others were just not for me, some are a great fit, and all have been a part of my journey of self-discovery and healing.

Are your inner and outer worlds filled with clanging and clatter? What if you had tools that effectively changed the station, so to speak, to something more soothing? Here are a few suggestions from my go-to list: intentional journaling, breathwork, walking in nature, meditation, affirmations, yoga asana, yoga nidra, disconnect from technology for thirty minutes each day, and two hours before bedtime.

Breakthrough

Intention: I think I'm going to be okay
Release: Thinking otherwise

"Major breakthroughs often come after major breakdowns."

–Matshona Dhliwayo

I have practices and people that support me. I don't take that fact for granted, as I have sought them out and sacrificed for them. They are my tools of the trade for daily living. By living, I mean living in the present, being connected within my own being, and having awareness of my connection with all living things.

I recently experienced a breakdown. It was a surreal few days where I felt the heaviness and overwhelm in my bones and in my soul. There was weariness in my cells from too much for too long. My nervous system was overloaded!

Yet, I was fully present for the experience, knowing it was a path I needed to follow in order to move forward. I stuck to my morning practice and my afternoon walk in nature. I journaled, meditated, repeated affirmations and mantras. I fulfilled the minimum life necessities and held space to be in it even though I wanted to retreat.

I've been depressed before. Many times, in fact. But this time was only the second with such intensity. The previous time, I was considering suicide. This time, dying was barely a fleeting thought. I have done the work (not that it's ever complete), and I have a great desire to help others. I don't want to miss that opportunity!

I had my first telephone counseling appointment yesterday as another tool to support myself. When we finished talking, I was halfway through my daily walk. I hiked up further into the woods, and as I gazed up at the treetops, I felt deeply grounded and connected within and to all living things. It was at that moment that I sensed a breakthrough and knew I was going to be okay.

If you are in the midst of a breakdown, only do what is necessary and let the rest go for now. Utilize healthy coping strategies and the support of healthy people. And always, always remember that your breakthrough is coming.

Connecting to Purpose

Intention: What is my "why?"
Release: Things that do not support my "why?"

Knowing our "why" for the endeavors we invest in can fan the flame of creativity and connect us more securely to living with purpose.

Taking risks feels much better when I believe in the project. This seems obvious, but as I take inventory of where I expend my energy in various forms—time, money, focus, etc.—I notice half-hearted ventures in the mix. This is not to say that everything I do must serve a higher purpose, but being a procrastinator, I can sink a lot of time into things for which I don't have a "why."

Being engaged with family and other loved ones is easy. Why? I love and enjoy them. Teaching yoga and other healing practices is a passion of mine. Why? By doing this, I take better care of myself, and I'm energized by helping others improve their health and relationships.

My newest venture is writing a book. Why? For me, it's another avenue to share my knowledge and what I have learned from my experiences in life. The hope is to encourage and support others through the difficult seasons, remind them they are not alone, and walk together on a healing journey. Writing is an extension of who I am and connects me securely to my purpose.

I encourage you to take a compassionate look at how and where you invest in your resources. Tease out the top five areas where you spend your energy and determine what your "why" is. Which of these five fan your flame of creativity and connect you securely to your purpose?

COLLECTION 18

Connecting

Pop the Lid

Intention: Find joy
Release: Weighty matters

We cannot avoid the sorrows and suffering of life, that is true. But if we are wise, we will take even the smallest steps to gather the fleeting glimpses of joy like fireflies in a jar to fuel our inner light.

I keep thinking that I'm moving forward, but this season of life is not passing through as quickly as I would like. I'm optimistic and back on task for a day or two, then BAM! I'm back in a mental and emotional slump. Honestly, it sucks! I feel isolated and stumped as to how I will find the wherewithal to endure. Yet there really is no reasonable alternative but to keep moving, so I must find new ways to cope.

I've always thought I was resilient, and I still believe I am. This floating in and out of being okay is not really something I'm that familiar with. In the past, when life has kicked me in the ass, I have sunk low and gradually made my way back to my feet. There is really no way for me to predict where life goes from here. It's more complicated. It's frustrating to try to generate business when I don't know if I can meet new obligations due to my son's well-being *and my own*.

Today, it's cloudy, windy, and cold, and I'm sitting in a coffee shop. It's the first time I've been alone and away from home in quite a while. It's the first morning routine I've missed with my son in months. I should be elated to be out kicking around, but I'm feeling the burden of the weighty matters of life. Maybe I just need to pop the lid off the jar—my heart—and run out to gather up a few fleeting fireflies of joy. I'm certain they're out there.

Are you weighed down by life circumstances and events of late? Just as there was joy yesterday, there is joy today, and tomorrow will also come bearing joy. It's there if you really look, so open the jar and let it in.

Centered

Intention: Be still
Release: Anxiousness

Note to self (and all who need to read this): Not every waking moment needs to be filled.

I have always had a good deal of energy and endurance. My strategy was to go like hell until I ran completely out of fuel and all but collapsed. Feeling mentally and emotionally anxious has a way of amping up the physical pace. I do this far less, but I have been known to drag my body around like an impatient mother pulling her resistant child by the arm. Keep up!

There is a price to be paid for not moving enough as well as moving too much. Whether you're inclined to curl up with a book all day or jam ten major projects into the day, balance is the solution. Whether we overdo with busyness or underdo with idleness, learning to balance the extremes is important for good health. When we practice being intentionally still, both mentally and physically, we get to know ourselves and our needs. We develop an awareness of the subtle energies within and intuitively know what is best.

The body and mind were not designed to be in a constant state of engagement or disengagement. So, whether your inner voice is telling you to keep moving or relax, you can discover your own truth and needs by being still and quiet and listening.

Symbiotic, Balanced Flow

Intention: Flowing engagement
Release: Too much space

To be simultaneously engaged in the energetic flow and rhythm of your soul and the universe is one of life's greatest gifts.

This is going to be a pretty busy week, and I will need to be focused and creative to meet my obligations. Part of me feels anxious, wanting to procrastinate and part of me wants to kick ass and take names. These are extremes, and I know I will be best supported and most productive by finding my own rhythm and then inviting the universe to support me in a symbiotic and balanced flow. Focused, yet open. Flowing, yet grounded.

Life is such an incredible array of options and possibilities. This makes me think about tourists who visit the vast landscapes of Wyoming and feel overwhelmed as if there's too much space. When it comes to focus and creativity, wide-open space can cause us to be distracted, lose our way, or even freeze in place. Too little space seems to block creativity. What we all need is balance.

Begin your days with practices that draw you inward and connect you to your inner rhythm. Check in with this connection throughout the day. If you discover your mind has been highjacked by wild monkeys, be still with both feet firmly planted on the earth, breathe deeply, and reengage in the flow.

No Censoring

Intention: Ask questions
Release: Fear of answers

There is an art to asking the right questions, and at times, an underlying fear of discovering the truth.

I've been completing several pages of questions for a course I'm taking. It includes questions that stumped me when I first read them. I skipped them and completed the easier ones, buying time to circle back around and contemplate my answers. One section cued to not censor your answers. This felt scary because someone else would be reading it. I shake my head at such a silly thought from a person who is writing a book. On second thought, I realize that my fear is more about what I will learn about myself.

My partner asks the best questions. They are like breadcrumbs, with each answer leading me to a greater realization about the issue at hand. When I question myself, I'm far more direct. I see that I have an opportunity to show more compassion as I delve deeper into my tender heart. There will be no censoring, just the purity of the truth of who I am.

Doing the deep work of knowing yourself is no place for being harsh. With each good question, we can slowly open the door to our true selves. It takes time. Leave the tough ones blank for now and follow the breadcrumbs. They will lead you tenderly to your truth.

The Right Tool

Intention: Grounding
Release: Energy of busy week

It's easy to become trapped in a cycle of busyness when you lack the right tools.

This week has been burning right along, and I am feeling it. I awoke tired and irritable, as my sleep was disrupted last night and this morning. When I arrived on my mat, it was obvious that a grounding practice was in order.

In the past, I could go through the entire day or even multiple days carrying negative energy and feeling like a victim of circumstances. It must have been such a joy to be around me! By the time my mood swung the other way, I had no recollection of what initiated my funk in the first place.

My morning practice is the start of sorting out where I am mentally, physically, emotionally, and spiritually. It's also a place to apply gentle accountability. When an imbalance is detected, I open my toolbox and find the right instrument. Today, I stayed low to the ground. First chanting, then breathwork, followed by meditation, and bringing it all together with a low-to-the-floor flow. I emerged feeling more grateful, spacious, grounded, and ready for the day ahead. The irritability? All but gone!

Do you notice when you have been swept up in the busyness of life? What are ways that you check in with yourself and hold yourself accountable? Write your answers in your journal.

Not a Grind

Intention: The work of manifesting
Release: Believing it has to be hard

I was raised in a family business. Hard work and long days (and nights) were the norm.

When I was just a few days old, my parents sold their farm in eastern South Dakota and moved to Fort Morgan, Colorado, to the first motel they owned. I was the youngest of six. My grandmother would tell me how she held me in her arms the entire drive.

Three short years later, they sold that property and purchased a new motel in Wyoming. This became our permanent home. We lived on the property—all eight of us. There were other ventures through the years and, as an adult, I returned to my hometown to devote my efforts to family business operations.

My parents worked hard, but we also had some fun and cool vacations. Still, business seemed to be weaved into all days and hours. Having your own business is not easy, especially with a brood of kids. Through this upbringing and my own experience running these businesses, I learned to value the energy it took to stay afloat.

My father passed away at the age of sixty-seven due to a stroke and my mother at seventy-six, after years of battling cancer. Neither was blessed with much time to enjoy their post-business years. What I learned from this is that I would have to figure out how to balance work time and personal time.

Manifesting is a whole different way of thinking about business. The greater work is shifting our beliefs about the process. Not everything has to be a grind! When we have the desire to realize a dream, something that we feel in our cells, the actions we take to move that dream forward are fueled by the heart. Of course, the work of doing is necessary, but if we are wise, we will hold space for believing and being as well.

Today's journaling project is going to be fun! Write down five things you would like to manifest for your business or for the work you do. Use two or more pages, leaving space to add updates to each intention.

For the next thirty days, read your five dreams upon waking and before going to sleep. Should you sense internal resistance or negativity, create an affirmation to use both in the morning and at night. More often is even better! At the end of thirty days, update your journal with progress notes, then continue for another thirty days.

Unique Gifts

Intention: Accept the gift
Release: Everything else

Each day comes bearing its unique gifts.

I'm participating in a writing "boot camp" today, and I'm excited.

Reading has always been a love of mine. When I was young, tall tales and stories would whisk me away! In my imagination, I would become a part of each. I read fiction books, like *The Black Stallion* and *Little House on the Prairie*. In my teenage years and into my 30s, my reading turned more to non-fiction for college and more practical purposes, like child-rearing, business, nutrition, and self-development. During that time, I dabbled in poetry and lyrics to express myself.

After my husband died from injuries received in a plane crash at the age of thirty-five, I needed an outlet for my grief. At thirty years old, I started journaling, at least sporadically. With four children aged seven down to three months and working, free time was limited, if it existed at all. As my children grew up and spent time pursuing their personal interests, I had more time to write, and I have filled several journals since.

For me, writing is a place where I feel much more at ease and thus, more authentic. It's a way to check in, be seen fully, express authentically, track progress, hold myself accountable, and move energy that is not serving me. And today's bootcamp is all about writing.

What unique gift has today brought for you? Invite your heart to freely release all else to accept and fully embrace it.

You Will Know

Intention: Trust
Release: Questioning

"As soon as you trust yourself, you will know how to live."
—Johann Wolfgang von Goethe

Each time I take my first step into a new venture, I am giddy with excitement. When I bump into my first obstacle, I begin questioning why I started a new venture. I question whether I have what it takes to see it through and if what I am offering will be good enough. The right questions can be extremely helpful, but those that cast doubt on my worthiness are a sure way to slow down or even halt progress.

My new project is writing a book. This book, in fact. I've always enjoyed a daily reading that gives me inspiration and a focus for the day. When I started the practice of reading and journaling, I was content to ponder the writer's thoughts. A few years later, I would jot down my own interpretation of the topic, which evolved to my current style that I call "intentional journaling." It's one of the first tools I share with clients.

Sharing my personal journal notes through the medium of a book is a whole new level of vulnerability. The fear is that I will be rejected by showing up as my raw, naked, and truest self. That aside, I have already made the decision to trust myself and continue writing. I'm all in and ready to charge ahead!

We all experience fear. We all question whether or not we have what it takes to live our dreams, and that's okay. We also know how to live this adventure of life as soon as we start trusting ourselves.

If you tend to talk yourself out of your dreams, know that it's okay, even normal to have doubts. But please, don't give up! Write your dreams down, read them daily, memorize them, and you will begin the process of believing in and trusting that you have what it takes to make them a reality.

Connected

Intention: Shine
Release: Low vibes

We are all connected, so when someone near us is vibing low, we feel it.

I spend hours every day with, or in the house with, my son. As he has challenging days, I am learning to hold space for him without being drawn in. Admittedly, I don't always succeed, but I am very aware either way. There are times when I'm the one in the pit and must take a timeout to reset. It's all quite normal.

Research shows that the electromagnetic field of the heart radiates three to four feet outside of the body. Scientists believe that this field carries information. I believe it, too. I'm grateful that this energy is a two-way street, but that can be a downside as well, depending on the energy.

If my son and I are both in a funk at the same time, it's a bit more work to switch gears. On the other hand, if one of us is shining our light, we have the opportunity to raise the vibrations of the other. Different emotions carry different energy. While positive emotions have higher vibrations, negative emotions carry lower vibrations. It's always fascinating when science catches up with our innate intelligence.

Take a moment to check in with yourself, especially your emotions. If you are feeling down, take time to breathe and move, spend time with someone uplifting, journal, or engage in another activity that will shift your energy. If you are feeling positive, let your light shine!

Express Yourself

Intention: Living authentically
Release: Censoring myself

I was just thinking about and reliving the sense of freedom I felt not so long ago. I'm reminded by this memory that there is something blocking that expansiveness now. I began to worry about performing, being successful, and growing my business. These are legitimate concerns, but they slowly crept in like fog and overshadowed my childlike wonder with what I was creating. Then, a major tragedy swept up the last remnants of uninhibited flow like crumbs from the floor.

I have been slowly building myself back up. Parting the curtains to let the light back in and cracking the window to clear out the stuffy fog. It's a frustrating process as if I had what I wanted, only to let it slip away. Yet, I feel gratitude that it led me back to the path of living authentically, spilling out on paper all that I have stuffed down deep.

Still, some of what comes up passes through a filter and is censored. Is it okay to feel this way? Will it make others feel uncomfortable? Do I sound like a crazy woman? The answers to those questions may all be "yes," but that's irrelevant. What's important is to create a sense of freedom again.

When you have been hiding, isolated, and experienced what you believe no one will understand, that means you need an outlet to release what you've repressed. You need a healthy way to process your emotions. Maybe writing is not your thing, so dance, sing, play music, bake, share your story, or support others who are suffering. The point is to express yourself and live an uncensored and authentic life.

Closing

"It is good to have an end to journey towards; but it is the journey that matters, in the end."

–Ursula K. Le Guin, *The Left Hand of Darkness*[11]

Dear Empowered Soul,

Thank you for traveling with me through the pages of this book! It's my hope that your journey has been remarkable, inspiring, moving, and a catalyst for deep healing and positive change. It isn't the end of the journey though, but the beginning.

The entries you have finished reading provide a format for your personal journaling practice. This style of journaling will support you in the most magical ways. I encourage you to read and journal through the previous pages as many times as you feel is right as you peel away the layers to find the truest, most authentic YOU. Choose the practices that resonate and make them a part of your routine.

You may want to transition to creating your own intentions and releases by following the Intentional Journaling format at the end of this section. Setting daily, weekly, or monthly intentions not only plants the seed of healing and change in your own heart and mind but also sends an energetic message to the universe of what you most desire.

While I do not know your challenges, I know that you have them. Maybe you are a member of "the call" club. Whether you have lost someone you love to death, divorce, injury, or breakup, or you are facing your own health issues or struggling to release the heaviness of other trauma that has turned your life on end, you can find the healing you need. Does it take time and work? Yes, but you are worth every second!

As you continue traveling and reflecting back on your life, I hope you are in awe of your younger self. Please give her credit for her incredible resilience and fortitude. Each of her experiences holds the potential to support growth and equip you to walk through trials with purpose and presence. Whatever lies ahead, have faith that the woman you are becoming will face it with courage, compassion, and intention.

INTENTIONAL JOURNALING

The greater part of healing is moving energy and taking the time to know yourself. Journaling is a wonderful way to move blocked or stagnant mental and emotional energy through your body. It is also a great tool for self-expression and discovery. I encourage you to create a daily practice of what I call intentional journaling. The following are the four topics that I suggested to keep daily journaling simple:

1. Intention: Write one to five words to set your focus for the day. (Ex. Self-care)
2. Release: Write one to five words of what you would like to let go. (Ex. Self-judgement, Other people's energy)
3. I feel ... Write one or more words that describe your emotions. (Ex. frustrated, excited, worried). Use a list of emotions to help you learn what you are truly feeling and remember the temporary nature of emotions. Such lists are easily found online.
4. Gratitude: Write down three things (or more) for which you are grateful.

There is no drop off between beginnings and endings. They are connected by transitions. The past, the transition, and the present are endlessly connected like links in a chain. Each occurrence of a beginning forms a new link, shifting our focus from what was to what is. As we release the past and transition to the next beginning, the chain continues to grow.

ABOUT THE AUTHOR

Kathryn grew up in a wonderful, loving, hardworking family in the Black Hills of Wyoming. Living in the midst of such beauty made her a lover of the great outdoors, trees, wildlife, fresh air, and the homey comfort of rural America. Following ten years of living in Arizona and experiencing college, marriage, and starting a family, she returned to her home in the hills.

After twelve years of working in the field of substance abuse and suicide prevention as a Certified Prevention Specialist, she started her own business with the intent to help others heal and live with empowerment using holistic practices. She has over 800 hours of training as a yoga teacher (registered RYT500, ERYT200, YACEP with Yoga Alliance) and is a reiki practitioner. More recently, she completed the Menstruation Leadership Program with Red School, acquiring more tools to help women work with the cycles of menstruation, menopause, and post-menopause.

Currently, she offers yoga classes locally. In-person and virtual sessions and programs with combined healing modalities for the mind, body, and soul are available to individuals and groups. She is also the primary caregiver to her recently disabled son.

She resides in Sundance, Wyoming with her PFL (partner for life), her youngest son, fourteen hens, and one rooster fondly called Big Daddy. She is the mother of four and a grandmother to two amazing children.

Visit kathryncluff.com to learn more about Kathryn's healing services for women and kick off your healing journey by scheduling a complimentary virtual discovery session.

For monthly inspiration, sign up to receive her newsletter and be the first to know about events and future books. You can also follow her on Facebook @soulrootswellness and Instagram @soulrootsllc.

Bibliography

1. Ruiz, Don Miguel. 1997. *The Four Agreements: A Practical Guide to Personal Freedom*. San Rafael, Ca: Amber-Allen.
2. Hanh, T. N. (n.d.). Stopping, calming, resting, healing - applied Buddhism. https://appliedbuddhism.org/th/mindfulness-practices/foundation-of-mindfulness/234-stopping-calming-resting-healing
3. Pope, Alexandra, and Sjanie Hugo Wurlitzer. 2022. *Wise Power.* Hay House, Inc.
4. Pope, Alexandra, and Sjanie Hugo Wurlitzer. 2017. *Wild Power: Discover the Magic of Your Menstrual Cycle and Awaken the Feminine Path to Power*. Carlsbad, California: Hay House.
5. Clear, James. 2018. *Atomic Habits: An Easy & Proven Way to Build Good Habits & Break Bad Ones*. New York: Avery, An Imprint Of Penguin Random House.
6. Bible Society. 1997. *CEV Bible.* Swindon, Wiltshire: Bible Society, Cop.
7. Chubb, Tanaaz. 2018. *My Pocket Mantras.* Simon and Schuster.
8. Don Miguel Ruiz, Don Jose Ruiz, and Janet Mills. 2010. *The Fifth Agreement*. Amber-Allen Publishing.

9. Keating, Joshua. 2013. "Why Time Is a Social Construct." Smithsonian. Smithsonian.com. 2013. https://www.smithsonianmag.com/science-nature/why-time-is-a-social-construct-164139110/.

10. Thompson, Hunter S, and Douglas Brinkley. 1997. *The Proud Highway : Saga of a Desperate Southern Gentleman, 1955-1967.* New York: Ballantine Books.

11. Le Guin, Ursula K. 2000. *The Left Hand of Darkness.* Penguin.

www.ingramcontent.com/pod-product-compliance
Lightning Source LLC
Chambersburg PA
CBHW071717120626
46550CB00001B/271

* 9 7 9 8 9 9 0 9 9 4 0 0 3 *